BestMasters

Mit „BestMasters“ zeichnet Springer die besten Masterarbeiten aus, die an renommierten Hochschulen in Deutschland, Österreich und der Schweiz entstanden sind. Die mit Höchstnote ausgezeichneten Arbeiten wurden durch Gutachter zur Veröffentlichung empfohlen und behandeln aktuelle Themen aus unterschiedlichen Fachgebieten der Naturwissenschaften, Psychologie, Technik und Wirtschaftswissenschaften. Die Reihe wendet sich an Praktiker und Wissenschaftler gleichermaßen und soll insbesondere auch Nachwuchswissenschaftlern Orientierung geben.

Springer awards „BestMasters“ to the best master's theses which have been completed at renowned Universities in Germany, Austria, and Switzerland. The studies received highest marks and were recommended for publication by supervisors. They address current issues from various fields of research in natural sciences, psychology, technology, and economics. The series addresses practitioners as well as scientists and, in particular, offers guidance for early stage researchers.

More information about this series at http://www.springer.com/series/13198

Helena Hartmann

Social Interactions in Autism

Cognitive Empathy, Egocentricity and Social Pain

Springer

Helena Hartmann
Institut für Psychologische
Grundlagenforschung und
Forschungsmethoden
Universität Wien
Wien, Austria

This master thesis was funded by a scholarship of the University of Vienna (Förderungsstipendium nach dem Studienförderungsgesetz (StudFG) vom bmwfw finanziert) and partially funded by a WWTF grant (CS15-003) to Giorgia Silani.

BestMasters
ISBN 978-3-658-22012-9 ISBN 978-3-658-22013-6 (eBook)
https://doi.org/10.1007/978-3-658-22013-6

Library of Congress Control Number: 2018941832

Printed on acid-free paper

This Springer imprint is published by the registered company Springer Fachmedien Wiesbaden GmbH part of Springer Nature
The registered company address is: Abraham-Lincoln-Str. 46, 65189 Wiesbaden, Germany

For Christoph, Elisabeth and Jens – the
people I look up to the most.

Acknowledgements

First, I would like to thank Giorgia Silani for the amazing opportunity to take part in such important large-scale research as well as for her ongoing support, encouragement and knowledge throughout the whole project. I am also very grateful to have had a qualified scanner user as dedicated, helpful and physically available as Lukas Lengersdorff.

I would further like to acknowledge the proud number of 50 (!) confederates who helped us realize our study design and made every single session more believable for the participants. In addition, I thank Kasimir Binder, Anna Cholewa and Yannik Thelen for valuable comments on the manuscript of this thesis.

Lastly, I am truly thankful for having been able to work together with my very engaged and valuable colleague Hannah Hitz, who was always there when complications arose.
I couldn't have wished for a better "confederate" than you!

Table of Contents

List of Abbreviations

ACC	Anterior cingulate cortex
AI	Anterior insula
AQ	Autism-Spectrum-Quotient
AQ-K	Autism-Spectrum-Quotient (Short form)
ASD	Autism-Spectrum-Disorder
BDI-II	Beck-Depression-Inventory II
BOLD	Blood-oxygen-level-dependent
CN	Caudate nucleus
dlPFC	Dorsolateral prefrontal cortex
DOa	Double Other active condition of Cyberball
DOp	Double Other passive condition of Cyberball
DS	Double Self condition of Cyberball
DSM	Diagnostical and Statistical Manual of Mental Disorders
EEB	Emotional Egocentricity Bias
EX	Exclusion
fMRI	functional Magnetic Resonance Imaging
GLM	General linear model
IFG	Inferior frontal gyrus
IN	Inclusion
IRI	Interpersonal-Reactivity-Index
MCC	Medial cingulate cortex
MFG	Middle frontal gyrus
OFC	Orbitofrontal cortex
PC	Precuneus
PCC	Posterior cingulate cortex
rTMS	repetitive Transcranial Magnetic Stimulation
SMG	Supramarginal gyrus
SOD	Self-other distinction
TAS-20	Toronto-Alexithymia-Scale-20
TE	Echo time
ToM	Theory of Mind
TP	Temporal pole
TPJ	Temporoparietal junction
TR	Repetition time

List of Figures

List of Tables

Abstract

Empathy, the ability to feel with another person, has already been widely studied in both neurotypical as well as psychiatric populations. In this context, the cognitive ability for Self-Other Distinction (SOD) plays an essential role during social interactions, mainly because it avoids confusion when one is confronted with another's emotional state that is not matching one's own. To be able to feel empathy, one must correctly separate and tag these self- and other-related feelings.

But social cognition skills are not free from error, since humans primarily use their own perceptions in guiding their thoughts about conspecifics. Such a self-projection mechanism can lead to empathic judgements that are egocentrically biased towards one's own perspective – an Emotional Egocentricity Bias (EEB) occurs. Since past research has shown that autistic individuals exhibit problems regarding cognitive empathy and Theory of Mind (ToM), they might also show more difficulties in classifying and distinguishing feelings of themselves and other individuals.

By means of the virtual ball-tossing game Cyberball, which elicits congruent and incongruent feelings of social inclusion/exclusion for the self and another player, we investigated (1) twenty neurotypical male adults and (2) fifteen participants with Asperger syndrome (AS) together with fifteen matched controls on the behavioral as well as neurophysiological level.

The results indicated a significant EEB during actively playing the game in contrast to passive observation, thereby showing that SOD is recruited to overcome egocentricity only when the self is directly involved on an emotional level. Interestingly, autistic individuals judged significantly more egocentric than controls when the degree of Alexithymia (the inability to identify/describe feelings) was kept constant. On a neurophysiological level, controls activated regions associated with affective empathy while observing another person experiencing social exclusion. Participants with AS, on the other hand, recruited areas related to emotion processing and mentalizing/ToM when confronted with incongruent emotional states of the self and the other. We found no enhanced hemodynamic activation in the right supramarginal gyrus, a region previously linked to "overcoming" the EEB, and no group differences. Nevertheless, the present study adds several valuable insights to the investigation of social cognition in neurotypical as well as autistic individuals.

Keywords: Empathy, Emotional Egocentricity Bias, Self-Other Distinction, Social Pain, Cyberball, Autism-Spectrum-Disorder, Asperger Syndrome

Kurzzusammenfassung

Empathie, die Fähigkeit des Einfühlens in andere Personen, wurde sowohl in neurotypischen als auch psychiatrischen Populationen bereits stark erforscht. In diesem Kontext spielt die kognitive Fähigkeit zur Selbst-Andere Unterscheidung (Self-Other Distinction; SOD) eine essentielle Rolle bei der empathischen Reaktion, weil sie beim Erleben von Gefühlszuständen anderer Personen Verwirrung vermeidet – besonders, wenn die beobachteten Emotionen nicht mit den eigenen, aktuellen Gefühlen zusammenpassen. Um Empathie für jemand anderen zu empfinden, müssen eigene Gefühle und die der anderen Personen richtig getrennt und eingeordnet werden.

Aber die soziale Kognitionsfähigkeit ist nicht ohne Fehler, da Menschen in erster Linie ihre eigene Sichtweise nutzen, um jemand anderen zu verstehen. So ein Fokus auf das Selbst kann daher zu empathischen Einschätzungen führen, die in Richtung der eigenen Perspektive verzerrt sind – ein Emotionaler Egozentrizitäts-Bias (EEB) entsteht. Da vergangene Forschung darauf hinweist, dass autistische Individuen häufig eine Beeinträchtigung der kognitiven Komponente von Empathie bzw. der Theory of Mind (ToM) aufweisen, könnten sie möglicherweise auch verstärkt Schwierigkeiten damit haben, Gefühle von sich und anderen korrekt zu klassifizieren und zu unterscheiden.

Mithilfe des virtuellen Ballspiels Cyberball, dass bei der Person selbst und einem Mitspieler kongruente und inkongruente Gefühle der sozialen Inklusion/Exklusion hervorruft, wurden (1) zwanzig neurotypische männliche Erwachsene sowie (2) fünfzehn Teilnehmer mit Asperger Syndrom (AS) zusammen mit fünfzehn vergleichbaren Kontrollpersonen sowohl auf verhaltensbezogener als auch auf neurophysiologischer Ebene untersucht. Die Ergebnisse wiesen auf einen signifikanten EEB bei aktiver emotionaler Beteiligung der Teilnehmer im Vergleich zu passiver Beobachtung hin, was zeigt, dass SOD als Hilfe zur Überwindung der eigenen Perspektive nur in Situationen gebraucht wird, in denen die eigene Person direkt emotional involviert ist. Interessanterweise bewerteten autistische Teilnehmer signifikant egozentrischer als Kontrollpersonen, wenn das Ausmaß der Alexithymie (die Unfähigkeit, Gefühle zu erkennen/beschreiben) konstant gehalten wurde. Auf neurophysiologischer Ebene zeigten Kontrollpersonen erhöhte Aktivierung in Regionen für affektive Empathie beim Beobachten des sozialen Ausschlusses einer anderen Person. Teilnehmer/innen mit AS rekrutierten dagegen verstärkt Bereiche für Emotionsverarbeitung und Mentalisieren/ToM, wenn sie mit inkongruenten Gefühlszuständen der eigenen Person und des Mitspielers konfrontiert waren. Es wurde keine erhöhte hämodynamische Aktivität im rechten Supramarginalen Gyrus, eine Region, die in vergangenen Studien mit dem „Überwinden“ des EEB in Verbindung gebracht wurde, und keine signifikanten Gruppenunterschiede gefunden. Gleichwohl trägt die vorliegende Studie wertvolle neue Erkenntnisse zur Erforschung sozialer Kognitionen bei – sowohl im Hinblick auf neurotypische als auch autistische Individuen.

Schlüsselwörter: Empathie, Emotionaler Egozentrizitäts-Bias, Selbst-Andere-Unterscheidung, sozialer Schmerz, Cyberball, Autismus-Spektrum-Störung, Asperger Syndrom

1 Introduction and Theoretical Background

One of the most unique aspects of the human mind is *social cognition* – defined as the processing of information in a social setting (Frith, 2008). By perceiving the thoughts and feelings of the people around us and empathizing with them in the process, we distinguish ourselves from other non-human species. With these innate perception skills, that are acquired very early and strongly refined over the life-span with each social interaction, we successively extend our abilities to better understand interactions in general and interpret the intentions and psychological states of our counterparts (Bernhardt & Singer, 2012; Lieberman & Pfeifer, 2005; Norris & Cacioppo, 2007). Lewis and Brooks-Gunn (1979) describe social cognition consisting of three major aspects: Knowledge of the self, knowledge of and about others, and knowledge about the relationship of the self in relation to other people. Interactions between individuals therefore constitute the basis for all self- and other-related processes. With the help of those skills, we are able to process incoming information in a way that eventually leads to relatively accurate judgements of other's mental states, intentions and feelings (Heberlein & Adolphs, 2005).

Especially in the last two decades, research in social, cognitive and affective neuroscience has been engaged with studying the underlying neural mechanisms of social behavior in the human brain, differentiating in particular affective interpersonal and higher-order cognitive processes (Emery & Easton, 2005; Singer, 2006). The former is represented by basic mechanisms for sharing feelings with others, a concept broadly known as *empathy*; the latter indicates mental states about oneself and other people (also referred to as mentalizing or *Theory of Mind*). In this context, the main focus lies on group-related and situational processes and on the complex facets of behavior that influence social interactions (Harmon-Jones & Beer, 2009): How are behavior, thoughts and feelings of a single person affected by the presence of other individuals or groups (may their presence be real, imagined or implied)? By combining social, cognitive and biological research domains with neuroscientific methods – e.g. functional Magnetic Resonance Imaging (fMRI) or Electroencephalography (EEG) – we are able to measure and observe typical human behavior in relation to its connected and underlying neurophysiological processes. Especially regarding the way that different kinds of emotions are processed

H. Hartmann, *Social Interactions in Autism*, BestMasters,
https://doi.org/10.1007/978-3-658-22013-6_1

and shared by various individuals or groups, the investigation of behavioral and neural deficits in sociocognitive processing occurring in many psychopathological disorders like Autism, Sociopathy or Schizophrenia constitutes a main concern alongside the study of the neurotypical population. This is most of all due to an increasing recognition of the differential characteristics and heterogeneity of socio-cognitive abilities and its diverse occurrence (Catmur, Cross, & Over, 2016).

In summary, by choosing such a multi-method approach, researches aim to further understand what basic mechanisms and networks in the brain underlie various social phenomena, how behavior and brain interact with each other to form how we think and act during specific social interactions and how social cognition abilities are represented in different subpopulations (Harmon-Jones & Beer, 2009). The present thesis tries to tackle all of these questions by investigating a crucial component of social interactions: Empathy.

1.1 Two Components of Empathy

Empathy, the affective and cognitive response that a perceiving individual experiences in relation to the situation of another person (Lewis & Brooks-Gunn, 1979; Shamay-Tsoory, 2009; Zaki & Ochsner, 2012), has been described as the foundation of matured social knowledge and presumably constitutes the most important principle by which we are able to cultivate, foster and maintain relationships to others (Lewis & Brooks-Gunn, 1979; Shamay-Tsoory, 2009; Zaki & Ochsner, 2012). Preston and de Waal (2002) proposed very early that the observation or imagination of another person's emotional state automatically activates a ("shared") representation of this state in the self, which is accompanied by matching autonomic and somatic responses. The ability of being able to feel *into* another person therefore forms a bridge between one's own cognition and those of the people surrounding us, even on a neural level.

In recent years, research has focused on the distinction of two components of empathic processing: *Affective* and *cognitive* empathy (Baars & Gage, 2010; Batson, 2009; Decety, 2007; Krämer, Mohammadi, Doñamayor, Samii, & Münte, 2010). Although the goal of these two components is ultimately the same – relating to another person's inner states – they highlight the difference between the affective-based skill of being able to feel what another person is feeling and the more cognitive skill of knowing and understanding what someone else is feeling, often in contrast to one's own feelings (Zaki & Ochsner, 2012). On the one hand, affective empathy constitutes a bottom-up simulation process that (often automatically or unconsciously) triggers the sharing of bodily or feeling states (Shamay-Tsoory, 2014). The mental states and subjective affective experiences of another person are reproduced in the observer as internal simulations, as if these states were experienced first-hand (Thirioux, Mercier, Blanke, & Berthoz, 2014; Walter, 2012). Cognitive empathy, on the other hand, describes a top-down inference process related to adopting someone's psychological point of view and deducing the correct affective state(s) through observation, while simultaneously appraising the situational context (de Waal, 2008; Shamay-Tsoory, 2014). It could also be called empathic accuracy, since the result is a (more or less) appropriate inference of the thoughts or feelings of a conspecific (Batson, 2009). As we will see later, the degree to which an individual can judge another person's emotions in an accurate way might depend strongly on the context and his or her cognitive ability to correctly judge the emotional state of that person.

But how is one able to know what another person is thinking? In the last few decades of the 20th century, the appreciation of elevated cognitive levels emerged under the terms *Theory of Mind* (ToM) and *mentalizing* (van Baaren, Decety, Dijksterhuis, van der Leij, & van Leeuwen, 2009). They refer to the capability of having complex and multilevel metacognitive understandings of our own minds and those of other human beings, i.e. wishes, motives, goals, beliefs and feelings (Baars & Gage, 2010; Luyten & Fonagy, 2015; Sebastian et al., 2012; Taubner, 2015). This encompasses conscious and unconscious cognitive as well as affective mental states. A fully developed ToM means that an individual can infer, understand and interpret the psychological or mental states of him- or herself and of others *more or less* correctly (Emery & Easton, 2005; Ickes, 2009). ToM can be divided into first, second and even higher order processes, which represent the different stages of intentionality that a person may exhibit in connection to the understanding of self- and other-related mental states (Emery, 2005): While first-order intentionality allows an agent, i.e. the self, to have and understand beliefs and desires, second-order processes give the agent the ability to have mental states about other agent's mental states. One's own ToM ability constitutes an additional contextual and social influence on the individual emotion experience of another's situation (Norris & Cacioppo, 2007). Especially people with a deficiency, an imbalance or failed integration of different mentalizing aspects, e.g. individuals with autism, might have general difficulties in imagining mental states and therefore face explicit challenges during situations of various social exchange (Luyten & Fonagy, 2015; Taubner, 2015). Although ToM is not necessary for emotional contagion and the automatic feeling into another's state (which roughly corresponds to affective empathy), it is a crucial part for understanding and classifying the experienced feeling state arising in the self (Bird & Viding, 2014). It is therefore partly represented by the cognitive component of empathy.

The complex network of human social cognition is supported by multiple systems of associated and interconnected cortical and subcortical areas (Baars & Gage, 2010). In general, (cognitive) facts about the world, intentions, beliefs and sensory representations seem to depend on dorsal and lateral cortices, while (affective) feelings, emotional values and social significances are most likely processed with the help of the subcortical limbic system. On the neural level, certain brain regions have been associated specifically with either of the two aspects of empathy (Decety & Michalska, 2013; Reniers, Völlm, Elliott, & Corcoran, 2014; Shamay-Tsoory, 2011; Singer, 2006; Taubner, 2015): On the one hand, ToM and cognitive empathy have been associated with enhanced hemodynamic activity in the medial prefrontal cortex (mPFC), the superior temporal sulcus (STS), the precuneus (PC) and the temporoparietal junction (TPJ). For example, regions in the STS have been found to be more active when tasks involve mental state attribution (Heberlein & Adolphs, 2005) and increased hemodynamic responses in the mPFC and STS were observed during the observation of drawings depicting people in emotional social situations (Krämer et al., 2010). On the other hand, affective empathy has been linked to regions in inferior frontal gyrus (IFG), anterior insula (AI), amygdala and medial/anterior cingulate cortices (MCC/ACC).

Next to the general definition of empathy given above, de Vignemont and Singer (2006) chose a more detailed description of the empathic process that better depicts the distinct affective/cognitive components: (1) A person is perceiving or imagining a conspecific in an affective state; (2) there is an affective response to another person's emotional state and in turn, affective sharing of this isomorphic state between the self and the other; (3) the empathizer has the cognitive mental flexibility to take the perspective of his counterpart; (4) the observer knows that the other is the source of one's own state and able to separate these shared feelings (i.e., self-other-distinction); and (5) some self-regulatory as well as monitoring mechanisms are present to modulate the inner state of the self. Damage to just one these underlying principles may ultimately disrupt the development of an accurate, fully empathic response or impair empathic abilities to varying degrees. Empathy can consequently be separated from other similar, but not identical, phenomena, that each fulfil some but never all of these criteria (see Table 1 for an overview).

Table 1
Comparison of empathy and related concepts.

	Affective experience	Affective isomorphy	Perspective taking	Self-other distinction
Emotional contagion / Affective empathy	x	x	-	-
Personal distress	x	(x)	-	x
Cognitive empathy	-	-	x	x
Full empathic response	x	x	x	x

Note. Adapted from "Social Cognitive Neuroscience of Empathy – Concepts, Circuits and Genes" by H. Walter, 2012, *Neuroscience, 4*(1), 9–17 and "Empathy: Its ultimate and proximate bases" by S. D. Preston & F. B. M. de Waal, 2002, *Behavioral and Brain Sciences, 25*, 1–72.

Sharing an emotion on the affective level without retaining some kind of self-other-distinction can lead to phenomena like facial empathy, motor mimicry, imitation and/or *emotional contagion*, where one matches his or her neural responses to the observed other through adoption of postures or (facial) expressions (Batson, 2009). When experiencing emotional contagion, the emotional behavior seen in others is mimicked and synchronized in the self (Decety, 2007), often without conscious or effortful control. During this automatic bottom-up responses, there is a complete identification with the experienced feelings without any discrimination between the feelings of the self and other (Bernhardt & Singer, 2012). Reactions like *personal distress* or discomfort can arise in the self if the experienced emotions coming from observing others are not regulated and controlled properly (Steinbeis, 2016). Personal distress is defined as a (not necessarily isomorphic) self-centered negative state that arises due to seeing other people in affective states and might hinder an empathic response (de Waal, 2008; Walter, 2012). But in contrast to emotional contagion, this distress is more self-oriented. Even though a distinction between self and other is made, the experienced feelings are falsely applied to the self.

Despite this, one also has to cognitively appreciate where that emotion originated (namely in the observed person and not in the self): This is achieved by consciously changing one's perspective, taking the subjective viewpoint of this person and being able to imagine what he/she is thinking or feeling (Batson, 2009; Decety, 2007; Lewis & Brooks-Gunn, 1979; Nickerson, Butler, & Carlin, 2009; Thirioux et al., 2014). This capability, called role or *perspective taking*, is closely connected to cognitive empathy (Walter, 2012). One must infer what someone else is "going through" and look for a representation of the same feeling states in oneself in order to understand the other person. At the same time, the self-perspective must be inhibited (de Guzman, Bird, Banissy, & Catmur, 2015). For this reason, explicitly representing the feelings of another person as a different agent requires more than just shared mechanisms, but additional conscious higher order representations and computational mechanisms (i.e. ToM; Bird & Viding, 2014). When we imagine another person's feelings, we always base this on how we think someone would feel in that situation or how we think we would feel if we were in that situation. The concurrent (and maybe most important) step in the empathic process is therefore to separate self- and other-related feelings and maintain this separation for the duration of the emotional state. In line with this, the American Psychiatric Association (2013) focuses on this crucial concept by defining empathy as the "comprehension and appreciation of other's experiences" and the "tolerance of differing perspectives" (p. 821).

1.2 Self-Other-Distinction and Emotional Egocentricity

Knowledge about the self and others is believed to develop simultaneously, because neither one is able to emerge without the common origin of social interaction (Lewis & Brooks-Gunn, 1979). Representations of the self and of others encompass the capability to distinguish between situations where perspectives or experiences are shared and therefore analogous between oneself and another person, and situations where they are different (Decety & Sommerville, 2003). The self is regarded as a multidimensional network that not only encompasses neural processes related to first-hand experiences but also shared self-other-representations. While the affective sharing component of empathy develops relatively early in life and automatically links feelings of the other to one's own feelings, mature empathy is only achieved through the development of a concept of oneself on the one hand, and the mental representation of the other person as a different intentional agent on the other hand (Schulte-Ruether et al., 2014; Steinbeis, 2016). In other words, both the knowledge of similarities and differences between self and other is crucial to feeling empathy and to avoid confusion of affective states (Decety & Grèzes, 2006). The correct and accurate evaluations of the thoughts, mental states and intentions of others and especially the decryption of their current emotional states are two of many skills necessary for getting along in social interactions (Norris & Cacioppo, 2007). The recognition of familiar emotions without verbal cues and inference of another's feeling state is facilitated, because the context of the social situation leads to a matching of the observed affective state of the other person with the help of one's own internal emotion concepts and knowledge (Heberlein & Adolphs, 2005). To react in an empathic way, internally generated or externally incoming information is evaluated, its origins acknowledged and "tagged" with the categories of self and other (Reniers et al., 2014; Thirioux et al., 2014).

This process has recently come into focus as the concept of *self-other distinction* (SOD). It is one of the recent focal points in the neuroscientific investigation of empathy. High SOD abilities have been associated with higher behavioral and self-reported empathy (de Guzman et al., 2015; Shamay-Tsoory, 2014) and its primary function is to avoid personal distress and confusion by the affective state of a conspecific. A few connected neural structures have been associated with reflection about and distinction of the self and the other, including the mPFC, the temporal poles (TP), the STS and the TPJ – areas also related to the cognitive component of empathy (Luyten & Fonagy, 2015; Shamay-Tsoory, 2011; Steinbeis, 2016). Especially the ventral part of the mPFC with its strong connections to the amygdala seems to be recruited during affective mentalizing processes. The posterior STS has been shown to play a role in visual cues indicating socially relevant content, like the perception of human bodies, body movement and the processing of agency (Heberlein & Adolphs, 2005). Further, both Zaki and Ochsner (2012) as well as van Veluw and Chance (2014) located the common representations between self and other during low and high level inferencing in a network involving the mPFC and the TPJ. Steinbeis (2016) and de Guzman et al. (2015) recently suggested that SOD recruits distinct neural sub regions of the parietal cortex: The posterior TPJ for the cognitive attribution of mental states and the anterior part, encompassing the supramarginal gyrus (SMG), for emotion-based attributions. The latter region seems to be especially important when comparing and categorizing self- and other-related emotional information (Silani, Lamm, Ruff, & Singer, 2013). The presented findings also highlight a possible overlap between self- and other-related processing, connecting these two viewpoints on a neural level and making it all the more important to cognitively distinguish between them in social situations to avoid errors.

But are we really always capable of completely distinguishing our own feelings from those of others or might we be naturally biased in some way? Lewis and Brooks-Gunn (1979) mentioned that already as infants we mainly use internal self-knowledge to guide our thoughts and ideas about others. These self-based thinking and feeling processes also persist and extend widely into adulthood (Steinbeis, 2016). Hence, during our whole lifespan, the mental and feeling states that one experiences in the self are the base for anything that comes from the outside world (Decety, 2007; Reniers et al., 2014). This holds especially true for affective states. The representation of emotions is very often focused on the self (Bird & Viding, 2014): The observer gains access to the state of the other through an unconscious activation of his or her own neural and bodily representations (Decety & Sommerville, 2003; Preston & de Waal, 2002). In other words, a great amount of the thoughts, beliefs, mental states or feelings that we ascribe to another person are predicated on our own experiences and representations first (Nickerson et al., 2009; Pronin, 2008; Singer, 2006; Steinbeis, 2016). In line with this, Decety and Chaminade (2003) suggest that the connection between self and other is underpinned by *shared representations* on the neural level. It is therefore not surprising that the default mode for processing other-related information has been suggested to be biased towards the self-perspective (Decety & Sommerville, 2003). This means that people primarily think or feel in an egocentric way and that it requires conscious effort to go beyond one's own perspective towards the (possibly distinct) perspective of another person (Decety, 2007).

Principally, we view others to be like the self. This view is based on the shared-representations-account, where individuals use their own cognition, resources and knowledge as a guide to covertly simulate the mental activity of a conspecific (Decety & Grèzes, 2006; Ochsner et al., 2008). For example, Nickerson et al. (2009) proposed the hypothesis, that the capability to empathize with other people at least partly rests upon the automatic tendency to ascribe their own knowledge and feelings states to them. In accordance with this, Lieberman and Pfeifer (2005) see empathy as a process of projecting the self onto the other person in order to better understand this person and his or her intentions. It therefore seems advantageous to recognize another person as similar to oneself and to correctly predict future behavior of others based on our own personal experiences. This egocentric process of viewing oneself as representative of others is also called "projection". And people are generally more inclined to consider the self as more representative with respect to others than it actually is. Many studies have investigated this egocentric bias in the cognitive domain, focusing on perspective taking abilities and mentalizing (Epley, Keysar, van Boven, & Gilovich, 2004; Epley, Morewedge, & Keysar, 2004; Royzman, Cassidy, & Baron, 2003; Surtees & Apperly, 2012). Findings include faster reaction times for judgements about the self and slower reaction times as well as an egocentric bias when judging other people's perspective (especially when it is not matching one's own). If this egocentrism holds true for knowledge about mental states of others, it is highly likely that the same also applies to thinking about emotional states. For example, the perception of a happy feeling state in other people is also dependent on how happy oneself feels (Goldings, 1954). Similarly, if the self is in pain, the attentional resources will mainly be focused on the self and everything else will group around one's own negative experience (Goubert, Craig, & Buysse, 2009).

While this egocentrism might help to correctly infer other people's emotional states and predict future behavior in some situations, it can lead to misunderstandings and misinterpretations in others. In this context, empathy research has focused on a phenomenon called the *emotional egocentricity bias* (EEB), which is defined as the tendency to project one's own affective states onto others and view the other to be more like the self in this process (Decety & Sommerville, 2003; Silani et al., 2013). According to Decety and Grèzes (2006), the accuracy in perceiving another's state is related to the magnitude of physiological synchrony: The required shift from one's own state to the state of the other and the subsequent sharing of this state might be relatively fast and easy when the observer and the observed person are in similar or congruent emotional states, but it might be a great deal more difficult when the experienced feelings are not matching, i.e. incongruent (Steinbeis, 2016). In the latter case, simulating another's emotional state demands the disregard of the own state in favor of the feelings of the observed person, i.e. SOD. Consequentially, if we are in the same emotional state as another person, automatic simulation processes help us to identify and judge the other's feelings more correctly if we use the self as a representative (Singer, 2006). But if the other person is experiencing an emotional state that is incongruent with what oneself is feeling at that moment, our judgement relies purely on mentalizing capacities or previous experiences and the own affective state has to be inhibited in favor of the other's state (de Guzman et al., 2015). Although Steinbeis, Bernhardt and Singer (2014) could show that adults possess a much smaller EEB than children when judging affective states incongruent to their own, even adults cannot completely overcome it (Pronin, 2008).

Scientists in the domain of social neuroscience have just begun investigating the underlying neural processes regarding those processes. Steinbeis (2016) recently argued that overcoming affective egocentricity activates a structure lying in anterior regions of the TPJ, called the right SMG. This was first discovered by Silani et al. (2013) who used a visuo-tactile paradigm that induced congruent or incongruent emotions in the self and another person by means of affective touch. In this study, the right SMG indicated to be crucial in overcoming egocentric judgements in healthy adults, because a temporary disruption of this structure by means of repetitive Transcranial Magnetic Stimulation (rTMS) led to a subsequent increase of the egocentricity bias. Steinbeis and Singer (2014) showed similar results with a paradigm targeting emotions related to monetary reward and punishment. In another study, Steinbeis and colleagues found that, with decreasing emotional egocentricity, the functional connectivity between the right SMG and the dorsolateral PFC increased in adults (Steinbeis et al., 2015). All of these results show that a functioning ability to distinguish feelings originating in other people from one's own feelings is critical for overcoming egocentrically-biased judgements in social situations, especially during incongruent emotional states.

1.3 Empathy for Physical and Social Pain

The majority of neuroimaging studies in the last few years have consistently shown that similar brain networks are activated when affective states are observed in other people and when those affective states are experienced first-hand, suggesting an at least partial functional equivalence of self- and other-related neural representations (Bernhardt & Singer, 2012; Corradi-Dell'Acqua, Tusche, Vuilleumier, & Singer, 2016; de Vignemont & Singer, 2006; Preston & de Waal, 2002). Empathy is typically studied in aversive emotions, especially in the domain of physical pain (Walter, 2012). One of the reasons for this is that negative emotions have considerable impact on individuals and induce strong empathic reactions because of greater emotional salience in contrast to neutral or positive stimuli (Reniers et al., 2014). For example, overlapping neural activation for first-hand and empathy for pain have been found in insular and cingulate areas of the brain, suggesting an embodied simulation of another's pain (Singer & Lamm, 2009): In a pioneering study by Singer et al. (2004), fMRI revealed that first-hand pain and the observation of pain in a partner activated similar neural structures in the brain (MCC, ACC and AI). Adopting the perspective of another person further lead to increased activation in the right TPJ. Jackson, Rainville, and Decety (2006) showed as well that both the self and other perspectives of pain activated similar neural networks (parietal operculum, ACC, insula). While the self-perspective activated somatosensory areas to a greater extent, the other-perspective yielded increased activations of the posterior cingulate cortex (PCC), the PC and the right TPJ. This supports the argument that representations of the indirect pain experience (observing pain in others) are qualitatively different but also (to some extent) similar to a first-hand experience of pain. Although watching another person in pain activates self-related processes, the self cannot fully represent the whole pain experience that is observed in others (Eisenberger, 2011, 2012). Nevertheless, observers somehow automatically resonate with another person, replicate the observed experience and activate a shared neural network in themselves in order to understand this feeling state (Shamay-Tsoory, 2009; Singer, 2006). This is an important finding in relation to the EEB, because it supports the notion of empathy originating from self-based representations of observed emotions. One then needs to separate arising emotions or thoughts from the feelings in the self and attribute them to the other person via SOD. This further aids in overcoming the egocentric default and imagine the pain of the other without being biased by one's own feelings. Interestingly, Decety and Lamm (2009) suggested that shared neural activations during pain and empathy for pain might not be limited to only physical pain, but could also be associated with broader pain-related phenomena like aversion or withdrawal. This leads to the conclusion that other negatively valenced emotions might exhibit similar patterns. One of those types of pain is of a social nature and has been suggested to be equally "painful" to physical pain (Eisenberger, 2015): Ostracism or social rejection.

Human beings are fundamentally social creatures that have a need to belong to social groups as well as a desire to interact and engage within others (Decety & Sommerville, 2003). People are always embedded in social groups, either bigger on a society level or smaller, e.g. peers, family and work colleagues (Heberlein & Adolphs, 2005). This existence inside social groups and the ability to predict the actions of other group members are based on and require social intelligence as well as higher cognitive functions (Emery, 2005). Complex social cognition abilities allow sensitivity for cues from conspecifics that might predict future behavior. Two fundamental needs that everybody searches to fulfil in a social context are inclusion and belongingness (Abrams, Hogg, & Marques, 2005). In contrast, humans fear rejection and being ignored or excluded by others (Eisenberger, 2012; Williams, Cheung, & Choi, 2000). In this context, *Ostracism* is defined as the act of "being ignored and excluded" from participating in social activity, often without a direct explanation or reason (Williams, 2007, p. 429). This form of exclusion is interpersonal, because it "refers to denial of access to a relationship" (Abrams et al., 2005, p. 18). The reactions to ostracism may be manifold and seem to diverge in current literature, ranging from self-doubt or loss of the self to specific negative emotional reactions (Abrams et al., 2005; Abrams, Weick, Thomas, Colbe,

& Franklin, 2011). Norris and Cacioppo (2007) suggested that both the perception of one's social belongingness as well as fluctuations in the quality of social interactions appear to drastically affect one's emotional life, cardiovascular functioning and health.

Williams, Cheung, & Choi (2000) put forward the idea that social exclusion can also happen without direct contact of the excluded and the ones excluding, and may be even more ambiguous because of missing (bodily or facial) cues that generally help to clarify a situation. They invented an online ball-game called *Cyberball* where people were made to believe they are playing with two other people connected through the internet (for a thorough description of the original game see Williams & Jarvis, 2006). Over the course of the game, the player was controlling a comic avatar and was either included in the game or excluded by not getting the ball from the others. The more individuals were ostracized, the more unpleasant and negative they rated their mood afterwards. Excluded participants also reported higher distress as well as lower levels of self-esteem and belonging, even if they were told that the other players were deliberately assigned not to throw the ball to them (Abrams et al., 2011; Eisenberger, Lieberman, & Williams, 2003; Zadro, Williams, & Richardson, 2004). With this paradigm, the authors showed the power and potency of social exclusion as well as its robust behavioral consequences, even in an artificially induced social environment like an internet ball-game.

In the context of research on empathy for pain, a similar negative reaction should arise when we see others being excluded. The perception, imagination or inference of another's negative emotions might elicit a reflective emotional state in the observer. Following this logic, we should feel bad when we experience a negative social situation in which we get excluded as well as when we feel someone else being excluded. A few studies have investigated the neural mechanisms of self- and other-related social pain through interpersonal exclusion with the Cyberball paradigm. Eisenberger, Lieberman, and Williams (2003) used fMRI to look at neural activations in the brain during this ball-tossing game: Throughout explicit social exclusion, when the subject was involved in the game but excluded by the other players, a dorsal portion of the ACC and the AI were activated in contrast to inclusion trials. The recruitment of those regions during explicit exclusion and an additional positive correlation between ACC activity and self-reported distress was also observed. Novembre, Zanon, & Silani (2015) compared neural and behavioral responses during both physical and social pain using an adapted, more ecological version of Cyberball with videos of real people playing the game instead of drawn comic avatars. Their results indicated strong aversive reactions and similar activation patterns for both first-hand as well as empathy for social exclusion. In line with this, it has been suggested that empathy for another's suffering might be reached via two routes: A "low", more automatic route, where the pain of another person is directly shown through pictures or videos or can be inferred via facial and bodily cues, and a "high", more cognitive route, where the empathic response is triggered by top-down inferences based on situational or contextual information that is often not visible (Bird & Viding, 2014; Walter, 2012). We see that another person is not getting the ball anymore and conclude that he might be feeling excluded, i.e. more negative in contrast to when that person was getting the ball. The other's state is therefore represented in the perceptual and cognitive systems of the empathizer. The Cyberball paradigm as a measure of social exclusion can therefore be classified as a subtler, less direct form of measuring pain-related empathy, because the pain cannot be directly seen but has to be inferred – tapping into ToM and mentalizing abilities (Williams & Jarvis, 2006).

1.4 Cyber-Ostracism and Egocentricity in Autism

A lot of scientific evidence for empathic sharing and processing of other's mental states comes from autism research (Norris & Cacioppo, 2007; Preston & de Waal, 2002). *Autism-Spectrum-Disorder* (ASD) is a psychological and neurodevelopmental condition that primarily affects limbic brain structures and has profound effects on personality and social interaction (Lai, Lombardo, & Baron-Cohen, 2014). According to the fourth edition of the Diagnostic and Statistical Manual of Mental Disorders (DSM-IV), the diagnosis of an *Autistic Disorder* is based on qualitative impairments in the following triad: Social communication, social interaction and repetitive behavior or obsessive interests (American Psychiatric

Association, 2000)[1]. Autistic individuals diagnosed with the *Asperger syndrome* (AS) often display no delay in cognitive or language abilities in contrast to people with infantile autism. These main social and communication difficulties of autistic individuals may be reflected in specific social cognition deficits traceable to underlying brain regions (Baron-Cohen, 2005). In turn, people in the autistic spectrum might react emotionally to their environment and to other people, but this experience could be qualitatively distinct (Preston & de Waal, 2002). While the view that empathy is generally disrupted in autism persisted for a long time, some authors have proposed different lines of reasoning to answer the following questions: (1) What parts of empathy are impaired in autism and (2) why is this the case? Firstly, research has again underlined the distinction between the cognitive and affective components of empathy to study dissociable mechanisms in ASD. A new claim, the so called "empathy imbalance hypothesis", emerged that just one of those two components is in fact impaired, namely the cognitive aspect (Smith, 2008). A lot of studies could indeed show that mentalizing and ToM processing seem to be the core of social communication deficits in autism (Dziobek et al., 2008; Mazza et al., 2014; Rogers, Dziobek, Hassenstab, Wolf, & Convit, 2007; Singer, 2006; van Veluw & Chance, 2014). Severe forms of ASD have even been characterized as "mind-blindness – an inability to accurately infer, or perhaps even to recognize the existence of, other people's thoughts and feelings" (Ickes, 2009, p. 60). Likewise, Baron-Cohen (2005) proposed specific deficits in the empathizing process, generally encompassing the capability to attribute mental states to the self and to others. On the other hand, the affective component of empathy seems to be typically developed in individuals with ASD: Dziobek et al. (2008), for example, found impairments in cognitive empathy (inferring a mental state), but not in affective empathy (feeling into another person) in people with AS.

Autistic individuals could therefore have a normally developed self-awareness and emotional processing, but fail to understand other's states in relation to their own. If people with ASD lack the ability to understand that

---

1 The 5th version of the Diagnostic and Statistical Manual of Mental Disorders (DSM-5) was published in 2013, creating one single diagnosis of Autism-Spectrum-Disorder with different severity levels (see Lai et al., 2014 for an overview). In the context of this thesis, however, these subtypes are crucial due to ethical reasons, since only people with at least average intelligence (Asperger-Syndrome or High-Functioning Autism) were invited to the study.

other people have mental states that differ from their own one's, they might consequently fail in the process to categorize and integrate emotional responses in relation to the other person (Preston & de Waal, 2002). This might result in misclassification and judgement errors regarding other's emotional states (van Veluw & Chance, 2014). It has been proposed that this so called "Self/Other Switch" (Bird & Viding, 2014, p. 523) is in fact impaired in autism in addition to problems with ToM, and individuals should show a stronger bias towards the self-perspective, because they are less likely to draw a sharp distinction between their own and other perspectives. A result might be increased personal distress or stronger autonomic arousal when seeing a conspecific in physical pain, because the incoming negative feelings are not separated from the self-experience and, in turn, are not classified as belonging to another person (de Guzman et al., 2015). As Gu et al. (2015) showed, participants with ASD exhibited enhanced autonomic signals (measured by skin conductance) when witnessing another's pain. The authors suggested that these dysregulated, heightened sympathetic responses further lead to difficulties in making correct other-related judgements.

In line with this, people with such socio-cognitive disorders should consequently show differential engagement of empathy-related neural systems (Zaki & Ochsner, 2012). A brief review by Di Martino & Castellanos (2003) reported that autism might be related to decreased neural activation patterns in brain regions like the mPFC, the TPJ and extended amygdala. In contrast, an increased activation seemed to be present in primary sensory cortices. Fan, Chen, Chen, Decety, and Cheng (2014) found preserved sensorimotor resonance (i.e. affective arousal) in participants with ASD to passively viewing another's pain, but decreased hemodynamic activity in areas associated with cognitive empathy and social understanding, like the mPFC. However, Philip et al. (2012) suggested reduced activation of areas in the brain responding to mentalizing (including cognitive empathy) as well as experience sharing (including affective empathy). Lombardo et al. (2009) reported possible direct impairments of SOD in autistic people: While neurotypical participants completing a judgement task recruited the ventral mPFC and the ACC only during self-related processes, these structures were equally activated during self- and other-related processes in participants with autism, making no distinctions between self and other. But exactly this distinction process is one of the most crucial aspects for overcoming one's own, egocentrically biased perspective when confronted with incongruent, conflicting emotions of the self and the other. In contrast to this, Hoffmann, Koehne, Steinbeis, Dziobek, and Singer (2016) recently found an equally sized EEB (using an affective touch paradigm) for controls and participants with ASD, but a ToM deficit was shown only for the latter group. This deficit was related to symptom severity of autistic traits. A separate resting-state analysis of networks underlying emotional egocentricity during empathy and ToM found that these regions seemed to be functionally segregated: While the right SMG was connected to regions associated with emotion processing (i.e. AI and MCC), the right TPJ was predominantly connected to areas of cognitive processing and ToM (i.e. mPFC, PC and PCC). Autistic participants exhibited disrupted resting-state connectivity regarding the ToM network, but typical functioning of the SMG network. Therefore, the presented evidence robustly indicates that people with ASD exhibit difficulties in responding empathically to another's pain because of a deficit in cognitive empathy/ToM. This impairment might be underpinned by a failure of self-other-distinction and ultimately lead to egocentrically biased judgements when being in a social situation producing conflicting emotions.

Secondly, recent studies have shed light on the importance of a subclinical condition that often co-occurs with autism spectrum conditions: *Alexithymia* is characterized by difficulties in identifying as well as describing one's own feelings (Lamm, Bukowski, & Silani, 2016). Highly alexithymic individuals are less able to form a conscious representation of their own emotional state. They might know that they are experiencing an emotion, but be unable to name it. Furthermore, they have difficulties in distinguishing feelings from other bodily sensations related to emotional arousal. This might be due to an inherent deficit in the ability to learn associations between cues regarding affective states of the self or others (Bird & Viding, 2014). Since studies have shown severe degrees of alexithymia in up to 50% of people with ASD (see Lombardo, Barnes, Wheelwright, & Baron-Cohen, 2007 and Silani et al., 2008), this condition should be taken into account when investigating empathy and emotions in general (Bird & Cook, 2013). For example, Bird et al. (2010) found no significant difference between people with ASD and controls in an empathy for pain task, where people rate the subjective level of unpleasantness of first-hand and other-related pain, when the authors kept the degree of alexithymia constant. Regarding the previously described shared representations of self- and other-related states, the implications regarding this condition become even clearer: If you have difficulties representing and feeling your own emotions, how can you accurately represent others' affective states (Lamm et al., 2016; Silani et al., 2008)? Bird et al. (2010) could show that the level of alexithymia (measured as emotional self-awareness) was in fact the crucial factor leading to a deficit in affective empathy and not autism per se. Furthermore, the inability to understand and identify emotions and the subsequent inability to empathize with others was associated with hypoactivation of the AI on the neurophysiological level. Lockwood, Bird, Bridge, and Viding (2013) compared the abilities for cognitive perspective taking and affective resonance in participants with ASD and showed a deficit in the cognitive domain which was not associated with alexithymia, but a negative association between alexithymic traits and affective resonance. This line of research highlights the importance of investigating alexithymia and autism routinely together in one study to dissect whether any found effects are a primary feature of autism or due to a high comorbidity with alexithymia (Bird & Cook, 2013).

1.5 Limitations of Past Research

In conclusion, the investigation of clinical populations associated with deficiencies in social and emotional understanding, like ASD, and their comparison to neurotypical individuals may shed more light on population differences in empathic processing (Bernhardt & Singer, 2012). However, the majority of prior studies targeting empathy and its components in autism have investigated mostly children or adolescents and the early development of ToM abilities (Mazza et al., 2014; Singer, 2006). It is therefore crucial to expand the current basic knowledge of neural mechanisms to a broader age spectrum of adults with ASD, focusing on general topics of social interaction and relationships to other people. Moreover, while a lot of research has been conducted on *cognitive* egocentricity (Epley, Keysar, et al., 2004; Epley, Morewedge, et al., 2004; Pronin, 2008; Royzman et al., 2003; Surtees & Apperly, 2012), the investigation of egocentric *affective* judgements as well as the neural mechanisms underlying this bias remain largely open or unclear. Especially the study of emotional social processes and complex social emotions on a higher cognitive level in the context of this disorder are crucial to gain a better understanding of the symptoms of people with ASD. While physical pain has been vastly investigated in this population group (Fan et al., 2014; Gu et al., 2015; Krach et al., 2015), research on social pain is been scarce and also centered mainly on younger age groups (Bolling, Pitskel, Deen, Crowley, & McPartland, 2011; Hartgerink, van Beest, Wicherts, & Williams, 2015; Masten & Colich, 2011; Sebastian, Blakemore, & Charman, 2009). Up to this point there is no evidence about the reactions of the adult autistic population to social rejection/exclusion of the self or about empathic responses to socially-induced pain. Especially the ability to distinguish self- and other-related states and the occurrence of an egocentric bias (in neurotypical as well as pathological populations) have only been investigated by few researchers up to this point and results are often inconclusive, ranging from intact to disrupted SOD in autism (Hoffmann et al., 2016; Riva, Triscoli, Lamm, Carnaghi, & Silani, 2016; Silani et al., 2013; Singer, 2006; Steinbeis, 2016; Steinbeis & Singer, 2014). Moreover, nobody has yet investigated egocentric judgements during more complex, social forms of pain by directly using a comparison of congruent and incongruent emotional states of observer and target. Furthermore, it has not been clearly established so far what role alexithymia plays in cognitive empathy in general, and more specifically regarding the ability to distinguish self- and other-related feelings during social exclusion (Bird & Cook, 2013). Lastly, research calls for more naturalistic, ecologically valid experimental paradigms to reveal alterations regarding neurobehavioral processes in autism, especially in the context of complex, multifaceted social emotions (Krach et al., 2015; Lamm et al., 2016; Zaki & Ochsner, 2012).

2 Research Goal and Hypotheses

The present study aims to expand current scientific knowledge about the neural bases of empathy, particularly focusing on socio-cognitive skills and egocentricity in the normal and autistic population. Following an interdisciplinary approach by combining behavioral and neurophysiological data in one paradigm, the present thesis targets to add valuable insights to the research on social exclusion and emotional egocentricity while overcoming the limitations of past studies and ultimately aims to present a more complete picture of differential empathic processing and the development of egocentric judgements in the brain (Zaki & Ochsner, 2012). A newly developed paradigm targeting simultaneously felt emotions in the self and others during an artificially induced social situation will help clarifying this essential ability to distinguish one's own emotions from those of others in situation of congruent and incongruent emotions.

This thesis encompasses two parts: The first study will investigate the occurrence of the EEB in a sample of neurotypical adults during empathic judgements of social inclusion and exclusion. Its major aim is to identify SOD as a crucial component for accurate empathic judgements by varying the degree of emotional involvement of the self and to show that SOD is only necessary for overcoming egocentric feelings when the judging person is emotionally involved in the social situation. The second study aims to shed light on differences regarding these egocentric judgements by comparing people with AS to neurotypical control participants. It aims at testing if it is in fact the cognitive component of empathy (i.e., SOD) that is disrupted in ASD and what role alexithymia and the degree of autistic traits play in this context.

In both studies, the neural structures underlying first-hand and empathy for social exclusion as well as self-other-distinction abilities and egocentric judgements will be investigated besides the acquisition of behavioral data. The described goals lead to the following hypotheses:

2.1 Hypotheses of Study 1

H_1: Simultaneous emotional involvement of the self and other during an interactive social situation leads to higher egocentrically-biased em-

H. Hartmann, *Social Interactions in Autism*, BestMasters,
https://doi.org/10.1007/978-3-658-22013-6_2

pathic judgements (EEB) in neurotypical adults, indicated by corresponding enhanced hemodynamic activity in regions linked to SOD, i.e. right TPJ/right SMG.

$H_{1.1}$: When participants are included during incongruent trials, they will show a shifting of their empathic judgement in the direction of their own state, i.e. more positive (Inclusion Bias).

$H_{1.2}$: When participants are excluded during incongruent trials, they will show a shifting of their empathic judgement in the direction of their own state, i.e. more negative (Exclusion Bias).

H_2: No emotional involvement of the self during an interactive social situation leads to lower egocentrically-biased empathic judgements (EEB) in neurotypical adults, indicated by a lower Inclusion Bias as well as Exclusion Bias, and corresponding reduced hemodynamic activity in regions linked to SOD, i.e. right TPJ/right SMG.

H_3: There will be a significant difference regarding the behavioral EEB and the hemodynamic activity between the conditions of simultaneous emotional involvement vs. no emotional involvement.

2.2 Hypotheses of Study 2

H_4: Simultaneous emotional involvement of the self and other during an interactive social situation leads to higher egocentrically-biased empathic judgements (EEB) in participants with ASD compared to neurotypical controls.

$H_{4.1}$: Autistic participants will show a deficit in cognitive empathy, indicated by a higher behavioral Inclusion and Exclusion Bias as well as lower hemodynamic activity in regions linked to SOD in comparison to control participants.

$H_{4.2}$: Control participants will show intact cognitive empathy, indicated by a lower behavioral Inclusion and Exclusion Bias as well as higher hemodynamic activity in regions linked to SOD in comparison to autistic participants.

$H_{4.3}$: These deficits in cognitive empathy/SOD (measured by the height of the EEB) increase with symptom severity of autistic traits.

$H_{4.4}$: These group differences in cognitive empathy/SOD do not change when taking alexithymia into account.

H_5: No emotional involvement of the self during an interactive social situation leads to equally low egocentrically-biased empathic judgements in neurotypical controls as well as participants with ASD.

$H_{5.1}$: Both groups will show intact cognitive empathy, indicated by no difference in their behavioral EEBs as well as similar hemodynamic activity in areas of empathic processing and no activity in areas necessary for SOD.

H_6: There will be a significant difference regarding the behavioral EEB and the hemodynamic activity within both groups between the conditions of simultaneous emotional involvement vs. no emotional involvement.

3 Method

3.1 Recruitment and Participant Sample

Neurotypical participants were recruited via flyers and email inquiries, media advertisement of the study in Facebook groups, as well as via the LABS-System (Laboratory Administration for Behavioral Sciences) of the Faculty of Psychology at the University of Vienna. Prior to the study, all interested participants were cleared for any risk factors concerning MRI by means of a thorough online questionnaire and further clarification of possible risks via email conversation. Only participants aged 18 or older without psychiatric or neurological illnesses that never studied psychology, didn't take part in a similar research project (regarding a pilot study in 2015/16, see Stepnicka, 2016) and had no risk factors concerning MR scanning were invited to the study. Furthermore, only male, right-handed people from Austria or Germany with German as their native language were enrolled in the study to avoid nationality, handedness and gender as confounding variables. For the behavioral part, six control subjects had to be excluded due to claustrophobia, below average intelligence, failed data transfer, technical errors during scanning and non-responding to the manipulation, generating a sample of $n_1 = 20$ for the first study. For the fMRI part, an additional two control subjects had to be excluded due to strong movement during scanning.

The second study included both left- and right-handers as well as males and females due to the matching of ASD and control participants. The autistic participants were recruited via an existing database of subjects that registered in the past for taking part in university studies, as well as by contacting institutions that diagnose and treat people with ASD in Vienna (e.g. Specialisterne Austria and Autistenhilfe Wien). Fifteen participants with an ICD/DSM diagnosis of the Asperger syndrome (F84.5/299.80) were matched to 15 neurotypical control participants regarding the variables gender, handedness, age and intelligence, generating a sample of $n_2 = 30$. The two groups differed significantly in their reported autistic traits ($t_{(28)} = -8.171$, $p < .001$). Twelve of the matched controls were taken from study 1, the remaining three were newly recruited. The total sample comprised $N = 38$ participants (see Table 2 for all sample characteristics and matching criteria). All participants were recruited and tested from

H. Hartmann, *Social Interactions in Autism*, BestMasters,
https://doi.org/10.1007/978-3-658-22013-6_3

September 2016 to February 2017 and scanning appointments were always scheduled during the week in the late afternoon or evening.

Table 2
Sample characteristics for the two studies and matching criteria for study 2.

	Study 1	Study 2	
	Controls only	Controls	ASD
Sample size	20 (18)	15	15
Nationality			
Austria	80 %	73.3 %	100 %
Germany	20 %	26.7 %	-------
Gender*			
male	100 %	86.7 %	86.7 %
female	-------	13.3 %	13.3 %
Handedness*			
right	100 %	93.3 %	93.3 %
left	-------	6.7 %	6.7 %
Education			
apprenticeship	10 %	13.3 %	20.0 %
AHS/BHS, no Matura	-------	-------	6.7 %
AHS/BHS, Matura	35 %	13.3 %	33.3 %
university	55 %	73.3 %	40.0 %
Occupation			
student	35 %	13.3 %	20.0 %
employed	55 %	66.7 %	60.0 %
self-employed	5 %	6.7 %	-------
retired	-------	6.7 %	6.7 %
unemployed	5 %	6.7 %	13.3 %
Regular medication			
no	100 %	93.3 %	80 %
yes	-------	6.7 %	20 %
Computer experience			
beginner	-------	6.7 %	6.7 %
advanced	45 %	46.7 %	33.3 %
expert	55 %	46.7 %	60.0 %

(continued)

Table 2
Sample characteristics for the two studies and matching criteria for study 2 (continued).

	Study 1	Study 2			
	Controls only	Controls	ASD	$t_{(28)}$	p
Age*	32.95 (8.51)	37.53 (11.03)	37.20 (10.84)	0.083	.934
Intelligence*					
SPM	7.70 (1.34)	7.27 (2.02)	7.60 (1.24)	-0.545	.590
MWT	28.65 (4.41)	29.53 (3.94)	29.00 (4.12)	0.362	.720
Autistic traits*	6.75 (4.75)	7.20 (4.86)	23.73 (6.39)	-7.265	< .001

Note. Percentages regarding nationality, gender, handedness highest completed education, current occupation, regular medication and computer experience as well as averages (standard deviations) for age, intelligence and autistic traits are given. The behavioral part of study 1 included 20, the neurophysiological analysis 18 participants. See measures below for a detailed description of the questionnaires. Significances of group differences in study 2 are indicated by the p-values. Matching criteria are marked with an asterisk.

3.2 Measures

3.2.1 *Social Pain and Emotional Egocentricity Bias*

The participants played a modified version of the computer-based, virtual ball-tossing game used in the study by Novembre et al. (2015) which is based on the original Cyberball-game by Williams et al. (2000). The version presented here used new videos with real people instead of cartoon animations, to increase ecological validity and approach a more real-life social context than in the original game. The new paradigm was validated in a previous pilot study (Stepnicka, 2016) and conducted as a measure to be used in the autistic population, ensuring as little distraction as possible.

The novelty of this Cyberball version consisted in the simultaneous emotional involvement of the self and another person to generate (shared) feelings of social happiness or social distress targeting the self or others. During the three here implemented conditions of Cyberball (*Double Self* = DS, *Double Other active* = DOa and *Double Other passive* = DOp), four players, including the participant, throw a ball to each other. The three conditions of the game differed in respect to the number of players playing (without the participant), if the participant was actively playing or only observing others play and whether the participant is asked to rate his own feelings or those of the opposite person (for an overview of the conditions, see Table 3).

Table 3
The three conditions of the Cyberball game.

	Conditions		
	DS	DOa	DOp
number of players (without participant)	3	3	4
player or observer	player	player	observer
rating of feeling state	self	other	other

Note. DS = Double Self; DOa = Double Other active, DOp = Double Other passive.

Every condition included 16 blocks of ball-tossing with approximately 13-15 ball throws per block. During inclusion (IN) blocks, the participant (the self) receives the ball from one of the other players and can throw it back left or right using the response box buttons in the scanner[2]. During exclusion (EX) blocks, the player may start by throwing the ball but does not receive it back for the rest of the block. Over the course of each condition, exclusion and inclusion trials are alternated and the congruency to the inclusion/exclusion of the opposite person varied: During *congruent* trials, the self and the other are both included or excluded at the same time (they experience similar emotions, either both positive = self: IN/other: IN or both negative = EX/EX). During *incongruent* trials, only one of the two is excluded from the game and doesn't get the ball thrown to him/her (they experience different emotions, either the self is included while the opposite person is excluded = IN/EX or vice versa = EX/IN). The order of the blocks was fixed (see Figure 1), however, the three conditions were played in a pseudorandomized order over all participants (resulting in six different order possibilities).

To measure emotional and empathic responses for social exclusion and inclusion of the self as well as the other, the participants were asked to rate

2 However, to avoid the empathic judgements being biased because the participant doesn't get the ball from the person he is supposed to judge, the participant cannot throw the ball to or get it from the person standing opposite of him (the other).

either their own feelings (DS) or those of the person standing opposite to them (DOa and DOp) on a continuous rating scale going from negative to positive (see Figure 2a) which was later converted to exact values between -10.00 and +10.00. The three conditions DS, DOa and DOp measure cognitive empathic abilities and the occurrence of egocentricity during incongruent in contrast to congruent emotional states. While the DS and DOa conditions directly assess the Emotional Egocentricity Bias (DS relating to first-hand and DOa to other-related, empathic feelings), the DOp condition (where the self is not playing) relates to a neutral, outside perspective with no emotional involvement of the self (see Figure 2b).

Double *Self*																	
blocks		1	2	3	4	5	6	7	8	9	10	11	12	13	14	15	16
congruence		Con	Con	Inc	Inc	Inc	Inc	Con	Con	Inc	Inc	Con	Con	Inc	Inc	Con	Con
target valence	**self**	IN	IN	IN	IN	EX	EX	EX	EX	IN	IN	IN	IN	EX	EX	EX	EX
	other	IN	IN	EX	EX	IN	IN	EX	EX	EX	EX	IN	IN	IN	IN	EX	EX

Double Other *active*																	
blocks		1	2	3	4	5	6	7	8	9	10	11	12	13	14	15	16
congruence		Con	Con	Inc	Inc	Inc	Inc	Con	Con	Inc	Inc	Con	Con	Inc	Inc	Con	Con
target valence	**self**	IN	IN	EX	EX	IN	IN	EX	EX	EX	EX	IN	IN	IN	IN	EX	EX
	other	IN	IN	IN	IN	EX	EX	EX	EX	IN	IN	IN	IN	EX	EX	EX	EX

Double Other *passive*																	
blocks		1	2	3	4	5	6	7	8	9	10	11	12	13	14	15	16
congruence		Con	Con	Inc	Inc	Inc	Inc	Con	Con	Inc	Inc	Con	Con	Inc	Inc	Con	Con
target valence	**self**	NE	NE	NE	NE	NE	NE	NE	NE	NE	NE	NE	NE	NE	NE	NE	NE
	other	IN	IN	EX	EX	IN	IN	EX	EX	EX	EX	IN	IN	IN	IN	EX	EX

Figure 1. Block order of the three conditions of the Cyberball game. Depicted is the block number (1-16), congruency (Con = congruent, Inc = incongruent) and target valence (always first for the self and then for the other; IN = inclusion, EX = Exclusion, NE = neutral / not playing). Source: Own depiction.

The use of these conditions served the purpose of evaluating the role of SOD in egocentrically biased judgements and if a failure of the first consequently resulted in a heightened EEB. It is important to bear in mind that, for an accurate evaluation of the other's emotions during incongruent trials, feeling states of the self and other need to be distinguished and the judgement needs to be independent of the own emotional state. During the DS and DOa conditions, the players should therefore show a higher EEB concerning their judgements because they are playing themselves (and are therefore in an emotional state that needs to be separated from the state of the other).

a)

b)

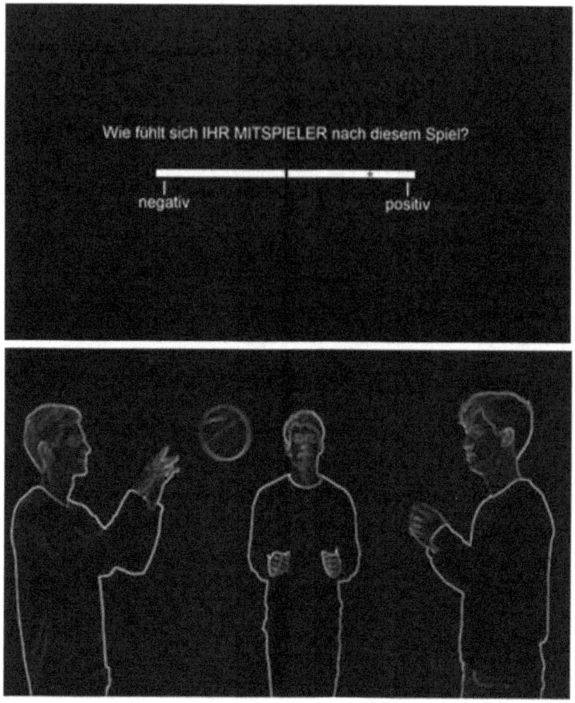

Figure 2. a) The rating scale of the Cyberball game. The participant is asked to rate either his own feeling state or the one of the person opposite of him. b) The Cyberball game. Source: Own depiction, game adapted from Novembre et al. (2015).

During DOp however, the subjects are not actively playing, but watching four other people play, and should show a lower to no EEB in this condition because SOD is not needed in a first-hand neutral emotional state. If, however, 2nd order theory of mind processes guide affective judgements of the other (e.g. "the included opposite player sees another person getting excluded from the game so he must feel bad for him/her and therefore also feel the same way as that person"), this condition should also lead to an egocentric bias. The present hypotheses focused on the comparison of the active versus the passive condition, while the differences between self- and other-perspectives was investigated in another thesis (Hitz, 2017).

3.2.2 *Sociodemographic Information*

Sociodemographic information on age, gender, nationality, highest level of education, profession, salary, living situation, relationship status, computer use as well as experience with computers and gaming was collected for further analysis. Handedness was assessed to ensure that only right-handed people took part in the first study and to match the control participants to the autistic subjects in the second study.

3.2.3 *Intelligence*

For matching purposes, two short forms of measures targeting general intelligence were given to all participants. The *Standard Progressive Matrices* (SPM; Kratzmeier & Horn, 1988) is a nonverbal measure to assess general intelligence with figural material. The used version contained nine items and for each, the participants had to select the missing piece to an incomplete pattern. Internal consistency values for the complete test reach Cronbach's $\alpha > .90$. The *Mehrfachwahl-Wortschatz-Intelligenztest* (MWT-B, Lehrl, 1995) measures crystallized intelligence and contains 37 items in total. For each item, the participants needed to choose which one out of five given words is in fact an existing word. For each of the two measures, sum scores were calculated to compare the participant's values.

3.2.4 *Alexithymia*

Since the presence of alexithymic traits needs to be considered and controlled for, especially when investigating the autistic population, the German version of the Toronto-Alexithymia-Scale (TAS-20) was given to the participants (Bach, Bach, de Zwaan, & Serim, 1996; Bagby, Parker, & Taylor, 1994). The TAS includes 20 questions that are answered on a five-point-Likert scale (doesn't apply at all, rather doesn't apply, partly applies/doesn't apply, rather applies and totally applies) and is divided into three subscales (*Difficulty Identifying Feelings/DIF, Difficulty Describing Feelings/DFF, Externally-Oriented Thinking/EOT*). An average sum score can also be calculated. An example item is "I find it easy to describe my feelings" [Es fällt mir leicht, meine Gefühle zu beschreiben]. Internal reliability coefficients for the three subscales range from Cronbach's α = .64 to .86. The cut-off score for alexithymia is a value of 51 or greater over all items.

3.2.5 *Trait empathy*

To measure the subjective empathic qualities in the participants, the German version of the Interpersonal-Reactivity-Index (IRI) was used (Davis, 1980). This multidimensional self-report questionnaire incorporates affective as well as cognitive aspects of the empathic reaction and includes a total of 28 items. The IRI is divided into four subscales, three measuring affective (*Fantasy, Empathic Concern* and *Personal Distress*) and one measuring cognitive empathy (*Perspective Taking*). All questions are answered on a five-point-Likert scale (never, rarely, sometimes, often and always). An example item is “I feel tender-hearted emotions for people that are not doing as well as I am” [Ich empfinde weichherzige Gefühle für Leute, denen es weniger gut geht als mir]. Internal reliability coefficients for the four subscales range from Cronbach’s α = .70 to .78.

3.2.6 *Autistic traits*

The Autism-Spectrum-Quotient (AQ; Baron-Cohen, Wheelwright, Skinner, Martin, & Clubley, 2001) is a self-report, 50-item questionnaire designed to measure the degree to which a person has traits associated with the autistic spectrum. Those traits are based on the triad of impairments (impaired social communication, impaired social interaction and restricted, repetitive behaviors or activities) and on other areas of cognitive abnormality. They are viewed as part of a quantitative continuum where a person can be located based on their score. The short form (AQ-K; Freitag et al., 2015) comprises a total of 33 items which can be divided into the three subscales *Social Interaction & Spontaneity, Fantasy & Imagination* and *Communication & Reciprocity*. The questions are answered on a four-point-Likert scale (definitely agree, slightly agree, rather disagree and definitely disagree) and a point is given for every answer recording autistic-like behavior. An example item is “When I’m reading a story, I find it difficult to work out the characters’ intentions” [Wenn ich eine Geschichte lese, fällt es mir schwer, mir die Absichten der Figuren auszumalen]. Internal reliability coefficients for the three subscales range from Cronbach’s α = .65 to .82. The cut-off score for a clinically significant level of autistic traits is ≥ 17. The AQ-K was used as a measure of symptom severity of ASD.

3.2.7 Depressive Symptoms

To assess severity of depressive symptoms in both study samples, the German 2nd version of the Beck-Depression-Inventory (BDI-II; Kühner, Bürger, Keller, & Hautzinger, 2007) was used. It utilizes 21 items to measure diagnostically relevant criteria for depression, e.g. sadness, pessimism, restlessness, feelings of guilt and worthlessness, suicidal thoughts, sleeping problems, etc. The items are rated on a scale from zero to three, with higher values indicating a higher occurrence of the named feeling, behavior or attitude in the last two weeks. An example item is "Sadness: I am not sad (0); I am often sad (1); I am always sad (2); I am so sad and unhappy that I cannot stand it" [Traurigkeit: Ich bin nicht traurig (0); Ich bin oft traurig (1); Ich bin ständig traurig (2); Ich bin so traurig und unglücklich, dass ich es nicht aushalte (3)]. Internal reliability coefficients for the questionnaire range from Cronbach's α = .84 to .90. The cut-off scores are set at 0-13 for no to minimal, 14-19 for mild, 20-28 for moderate and 29 or higher for severe depressive symptoms.

3.2.8 Paradigm Believability

To assess believability regarding the manipulation, participants were asked during the debriefing how involved they had felt in the game with the other players. If the participant noted, they hadn't believed they were playing with others, they were further asked, from which point on first doubts arose (during the instruction, during one of the three games or after the scanning) and if the participants had "felt" emotions during situations of inclusion and exclusion regardless of believing in the manipulation[3].

3.3 fMRI Design and Study Procedure

MRI data was acquired using a 3-Tesla Siemens Magnetom Skyra MRI-system (Siemens Medical, Erlangen, Germany) at the university dental clinic in Vienna, equipped with a 32-channel head coil and a high-performance gradient system for fast, high-resolution whole-brain multiband

3 Regarding the neurobehavioral investigation of social pain in general, and especially because of this increased uncertainty of emotional states in a paradigm such as Cyberball, it is important to always assess subjective experiences in response to the exclusion and in particular, whether the subjects actually believed they were being rejected (Eisenberger, 2015a).

echoplanar imaging. The scanning sequence included the following parameters: Echo time (TE) / repetition time (TR) = 34/704 ms, flip angle = 50°, interleaved acquisition, interleaved multi-slice mode, 32 axial slices coplanar the connecting line between anterior and posterior commissure, slice thickness = 3.5 mm, field of view = 210 mm, matrix size = 96×96, voxel size = 2.2×2.2×3.5 mm. For each of the three conditions, about ~1070 volumes were acquired within one run with durations ranging from 11 to 13 min per run. Structural images were acquired after functional scanning using a magnetization-prepared rapid gradient-echo sequence (TE/TR = 2.29/2300 ms, 176 sagittal slices, voxel size = 0.9×0.9×0.9 mm, flip angle = 8°, ascending acquisition, single shot multi-slice mode, slice thickness = 0.94 mm, field of view = 240 mm)[4]. Total scanning time lasted about 60 min including small breaks between the different runs.

The study procedure took an average of two and a half hours for every participant and consisted of a single session. After arranging an appointment via email, the participant was sent information about the study and magnetic resonance imaging. He/she was asked not to take any medication, drugs or alcohol 24 hours prior to the appointment. In the email, the participant was told that he/she would be taking part in the study with four other participants (that had been recruited separately from the "scanner participants") and that he/she would be the only one lying in the scanner. The other participants were in fact confederates used to make the social situation of the virtual ballgame more realistic and to make the participant believe that he/she was playing with other people. The confederates were instructed prior to the study to act as naive study participants. There were always two different female and two different male confederates present for every session. After picking the participant and the four confederates up from the meeting-point, they were brought into the scanning area, where five computers were already set up. One of the two test administrators took the scanner participant outside to fill out and sign two fMRI-safety questionnaires to check again for MR-related risks (i.e. metal in the

4 Gradient field maps were also acquired after the game, but these were not used in the subsequent analysis of the fMRI data. The following parameters were employed: TE/TR = 4.92/400 ms, 36 slices, voxel size = 1.7×1.7×3.5 mm, flip angle = 60°, interleaved acquisition, interleaved multi-slice mode, slice thickness = 3.5 mm, field of view = 220 mm, series = interleaved.

body, claustrophobia and neurological illnesses). These safety questions were asked verbally by the test administrator to ensure that the participant correctly understood and answered all questions. Every participant received the before sent information sheet about the study and had the possibility to ask remaining questions. Meanwhile, the second test administrator sat in the scanning area with the other four participants and handed out the study information sheets to read. Everybody signed the informed consent before proceeding with the instruction of the task. Then, the scanner subject joined the others and the five subjects were given a verbal instruction of the Cyberball task, making sure that the participant(s) understood it. After that, all subjects were told that they would now play two short practice rounds of the game together on the computers and then they would play three full games with one participant lying in the scanner.

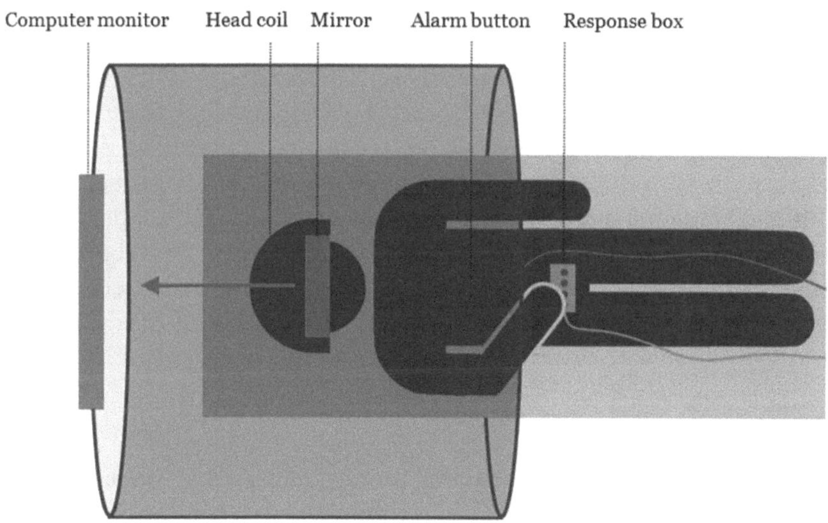

Figure 3. Setup for the participant in the MR-scanner. Source: Depiction from D. Pairitsch.

To induce a believable social situation, the participants were told that all players would be connected via the internet before the game started so they could play with each other simultaneously and because of that, they had to press enter at the same time to "log on" to the game together and facilitate the subsequent connection. After the practice rounds, the scanner participant was asked to remove any metallic objects and checked again by the qualified scanner user for any safety risks, while the confederates remained seated at their computers and were free to leave as soon as the participant was lying in the scanner. Following that were three runs of playing Cyberball in the scanner with the different conditions (DS, DOa, DOp) presented in a pseudorandomized order for every participant. The participant watched the game over a mirror attached to his headpiece and pressed the buttons of a response box lying on his thighs (see Figure 3 for the setup in the MR-scanner).

3.4 Statistical Analysis

The behavioral data was acquired and extracted using MATLAB R20.10a (MathWorks). All statistical analyses related to behavioral and questionnaire data were done with the IBM SPSS Statistics software (Version 22). Data analysis was performed based on a general linear model (GLM) approach. The hypotheses in study 1 (controls only) were assessed with a three-factorial repeated measures Analysis of Variance (ANOVA) including the two-level factors *condition* (active vs. passive emotional involvement of the self, i.e. player or observer), *valence* (inclusion vs. exclusion of the other player in the ball-game) and *congruency* (congruent vs. incongruent emotional experience of the self and other). To test the hypotheses in study 2, a four-factorial mixed ANOVA with the three above mentioned within-subject factors and the additional between-subjects factor *group* (control vs. ASD) was calculated. In a second step, the degrees of alexithymic and autistic traits were separately included as covariates.

To preprocess and statistically analyze the functional MRI data, the current version of the software Statistical Parametric Mapping (SPM 12, Wellcome Trust Centre for Neuroimaging) running on MATLAB was used. Preprocessing included realignment, coregistration of each individual's structural MRI scan to the first functional image, segmentation into gray matter, white matter and cerebrospinal fluid tissues, spatial normalization to the structural image, and spatial smoothing by convolution with an 8 mm full-width at half-maximum (FWHM) Gaussian Kernel. A ±2 mm/degree threshold was applied for excessive head movement. The first-level design matrix of each subject contained two separate regressors (video and rating) for each valence (inclusion, exclusion) and for each congruency level (congruent, incongruent), leading to a total of eight regressors for each of the three games (self, active, passive)[5]. For each condition, the entire time from the onset of the first Cyberball game until the last rating scale was modeled in a block-design fashion and convolved with SPM12's standard canonical hemodynamic response function (interscan interval = 0.704). Additional nuisance regressors included the realignment parameters. For the second-level analysis, a full factorial design with three within-subject factors condition, valence and congruency (study 1), and an additional between-subjects factor group (study 2) was implemented in SPM.

5 Note that the Cyberball condition *Double Self*, where the participants had to rate their own feelings, was used for analysis in another thesis (Hitz, 2017) and is thus not mentioned in the 2nd level analysis and the subsequent results. The present thesis focused on the comparison of empathic judgements during active playing versus passive observation.

4 Results

4.1 Behavioral Results

4.1.1 Study 1

The mean ratings and standard deviations of 20 healthy adults are listed in Table 4. When the participants were actively playing (DOa), they judged the other person's feelings more negative when they themselves were being excluded from the game (Exclusion Bias) and more positive when they themselves were being included in the game (Inclusion Bias). In other words, the participants shifted their empathic judgement towards their own emotional state when the self and other were experiencing incongruent compared to congruent feelings – demonstrating an EEB.

Table 4
Means, standard deviations and mean EEBs for the two conditions of Cyberball.

Sequence (S/O)		*M*	*SD*		*M*	*SD*		*M*	*SD*
DOa	IN/IN	4.69	3.46	EB	1.42	4.27	EEB	1.35	2.39
	EX/IN	3.27	4.00						
	EX/EX	(-)5.14	3.70	IB	1.28	3.96			
	IN/EX	(-)3.85	4.10						
DOp	IN/IN	3.56	2.72	EB	0.10	3.97	EEB	-0.22	2.07
	EX/IN	3.46	3.36						
	EX/EX	(-)4.82	3.32	IB	-0.54	3.01			
	IN/EX	(-)5.36	2.88						

Note. DOa = Double Other active, DOp = Double Other passive, S = self, O = other, IN = inclusion, EX = exclusion, EB = Exclusion Bias, IB = Inclusion Bias, EEB = Overall Emotional Egocentricity Bias. The sign of the EX/EX and IN/EX sequences was reverted to compare the mean EEBs to each other. The exclusion bias was calculated by subtracting EX/IN from IN/IN, the inclusion bias by subtracting IN/EX from EX/EX. The overall EEB was calculated as an average of the exclusion and inclusion bias.

H. Hartmann, *Social Interactions in Autism*, BestMasters,
https://doi.org/10.1007/978-3-658-22013-6_4

During DOp, when the participants were passively observing a ball-game between four other players, they did not shift their empathic judgement of the other person in the direction their own emotional state, showing no EEB (see Figure 4a+b).

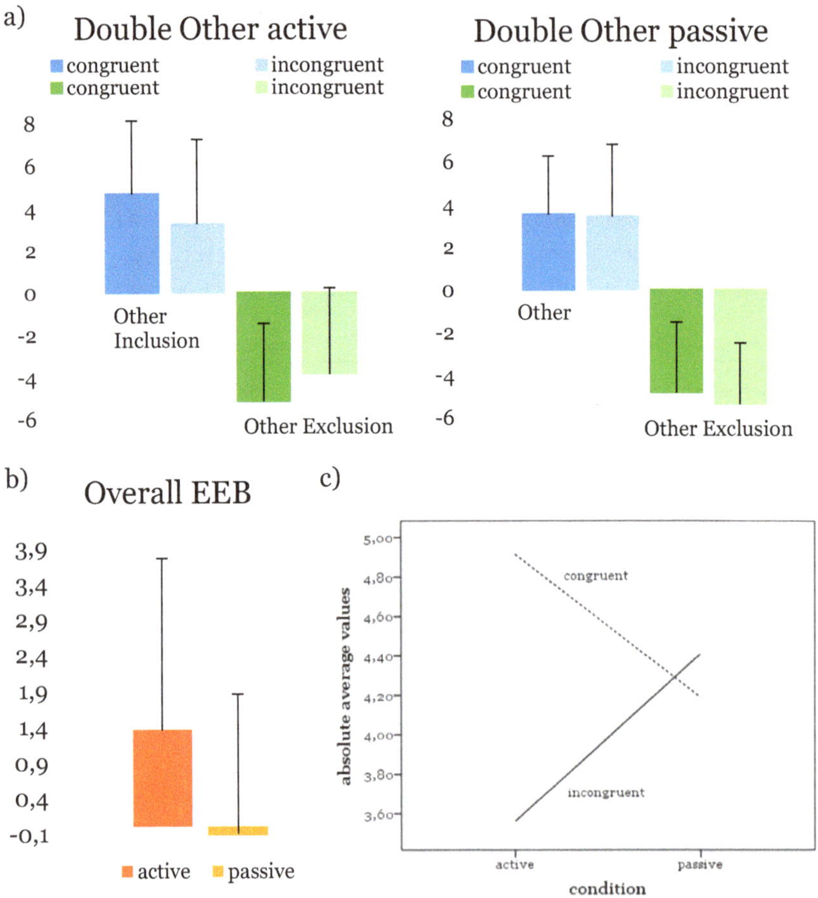

Figure 4. a) Plotted mean rating values and standard deviations of the conditions Double Other active (DOa) and Double Other passive (DOp) of study 1. Participants showed an EEB in their empathic judgements of the other during DOa, when they were actively playing Cyberball, but not during DOp, when they were passively observing four others play. b) Plotted Emotional Egocentricity Bias for the conditions DOa and DOp. c) Plotted condition x congruency interaction ($F_{(1,19)} = 12.281$, $p = .002$, $\eta_p^2 = 0.393$). Source: Own depiction.

A three-factorial (2 x 2 x 2) repeated measures ANOVA (GLM) was used to assess the levels of egocentric empathic judgements in the two conditions. To measure and compare the size of the EEB free of valence (bias either in the direction of one's own positive or negative state, see Figure 4a for the non-inverted data), the negative signs of the ratings related to exclusion of the other person (EX/EX and IN/EX) were inverted. A significant interaction for condition x congruency ($F_{(1,19)} = 12.281$, $p = .002$, $\eta_p^2 = 0.393$) was observed (Figure 4c). Planned comparisons via simple effects analysis revealed that this interaction was driven by a significant average difference between congruent and incongruent blocks in the DOa condition, where the participants were emotionally involved in the game (congruent – incongruent (*M*/*SE*) = 1.36/0.53; $p = .020$) in contrast to the DOp condition, when the participants were merely observing the ball-play (congruent – incongruent (*M*/*SE*) = -0.22/0.46; $p = .639$). In other words, during emotional involvement of the self, the participants judged the other person in a significantly more egocentric way (indicated by the higher difference between congruent and incongruent trials) than during passive observation without first-hand emotional involvement.

In this context, it should be noted that for DOa, the average empathic judgement during congruent trials was higher than during incongruent trials (congruent (*M*/*SE*) = 4.92/0.50; incongruent = 3.56/0.57), however, for DOp this was reversed (congruent (*M*/*SE*) = 4.19/0.51; incongruent = 4.41/0.50; see also Figure 4c). All other main effects and interactions were not significant (condition, $F_{(1,19)} = 0.094$, $p = .762$, $\eta_p^2 = 0.005$; valence, $F_{(1,19)} = 1.582$, $p = .224$, $\eta_p^2 = 0.077$; congruency, $F_{(1,19)} = 1.611$, $p = .220$, $\eta_p^2 = 0.078$; condition x valence, $F_{(1,19)} = 1.974$, $p = .176$, $\eta_p^2 = 0.094$; valence x congruency, $F_{(1,19)} = 0.087$, $p = .771$, $\eta_p^2 = 0.005$; condition x valence x congruency, $F_{(1,21)} = 0.283$, $p = .601$, $\eta_p^2 = 0.015$). The absence of a three-way interaction with valence documents that the EEB was of a similar size for emotions biased by first-hand inclusion and exclusion (DOa: IN Bias (*M*/*SE*) = 1.28/0.89, EX Bias = 1.42/0.95; DOp: IN Bias: -0.54/0.69, EX Bias: 0.10/0.89). To analyze separately whether the valence of the egocentric shift (in the positive or negative direction) was different within the conditions, paired-samples *t*-Tests were calculated. The results indicated that the Inclusion Bias and the Exclusion Bias did not differ significantly from each other in the active ($t_{(19)} = -0.093$, $p = .927$; Inclusion – Exclusion bias (*M*/*SE*) = -0.14/1.50) as well as the passive condition ($t_{(19)}$ = -0.493, p = .627; Inclusion – Exclusion bias (M/SE) = -0.64/1.29). In both conditions, the participants exhibited egocentric shifts of a similar size when judging the other person, either towards their own positive or their own negative emotional state.

Investigating associations of the mean EEBs and their difference in conditions of active emotional involvement and passive observation with different levels of alexithymia, trait empathy and autistic traits, two-sided Spearman correlations were calculated. The difference between the active and passive EEB was not associated with any of the scales assessing alexithymia or trait empathy, however, there was a significant positive association between the size of this difference and autistic traits (r_s = .45, p = .048): Healthy adult participants with a higher number of autistic symptoms showed a greater difference between the active and passive conditions and vice versa. This could have resulted either by a higher EEB during first-hand emotional involvement, a lower EEB during passive observation or both. The results further indicated a significant negative association between the EEB in the passive condition and a difficulty to identify feelings (r_s = -.65, p = .002): Less difficulty to identify feelings cohered with a higher bias in the passive condition (see Tables A1 and A2 in Appendix I for all correlational results and averages regarding the questionnaires and Table A3 for results regarding the rating durations).

4.1.2 Study 2

The mean ratings and standard deviations of the experimental sample with 15 participants with ASD and 15 matched neurotypical control participants (n_2 = 30) are separately listed in Table **5**. When the participants were actively playing (DOa), they rated the other person as feeling more negative when they themselves were excluded from the game and more positive when they themselves were being included in the game, as shown in study 1 (see also Figure 5a).

Table 5
Means, standard deviations and mean EEBs for the two conditions of Cyberball separate for the two groups (Controls vs. ASD).

Sequence (S/O)		Controls (n = 15)		ASD (n = 15)	
		M	*SD*	*M*	*SD*
DOa	IN/IN	4.20	3.45	3.24	3.34
	EX/IN	4.24	3.54	1.71	2.61
	EX/EX	(-)4.59	3.63	(-)5.39	3.25
	IN/EX	(-)3.30	4.14	(-)2.93	1.97
	Exclusion Bias	-0.04	2.20	1.53	3.77
	Inclusion Bias	1.29	3.91	2.47	2.24
	Overall EEB	0.63	2.32	2.00	2.50
DOp	IN/IN	3.60	2.93	3.37	3.84
	EX/IN	3.74	2.97	3.02	3.31
	EX/EX	(-)3.92	3.25	(-)4.76	3.47
	IN/EX	(-)5.08	2.92	(-)4.76	2.86
	Exclusion Bias	-0.14	2.91	0.35	4.04
	Inclusion Bias	-1.16	3.34	0.00	1.93
	Overall EEB	-0.65	2.52	0.18	2.70

Note. DOa = Double Other active, DOp = Double Other passive, S = self, O = other, IN = inclusion, EX = exclusion. The sign of the EX/EX and IN/EX sequences was reverted to compare the mean EEBs to each other. The exclusion bias was calculated by subtracting EX/IN from IN/IN, the inclusion bias by subtracting IN/EX from EX/EX. The overall EEB was calculated as an average of the exclusion and inclusion bias.

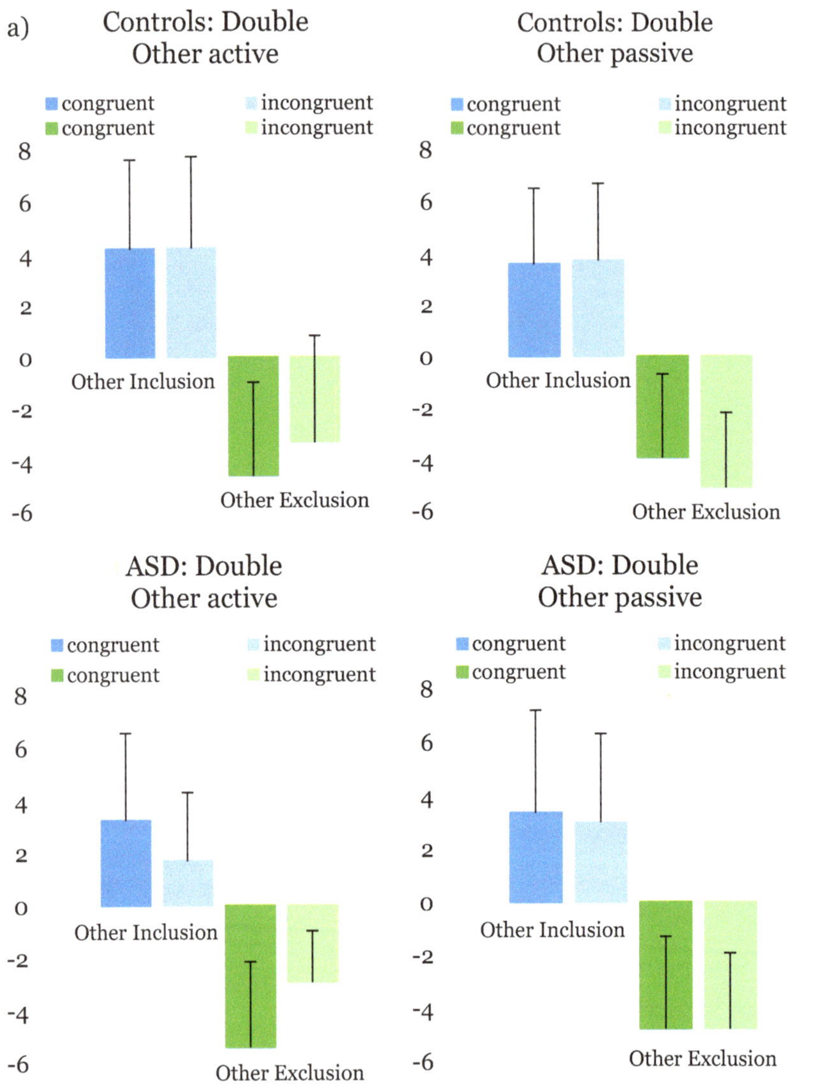

Figure 5. a) Plotted mean rating values and standard deviations of the conditions Double Other active (DOa) and Double Other passive (DOp) of study 2 separate for controls and ASD participants. Participants showed an EEB in their empathic judgements of the other during DOa, when they were actively playing the game, but not during DOp, when they were passively observing four others play. Source: Own depiction.

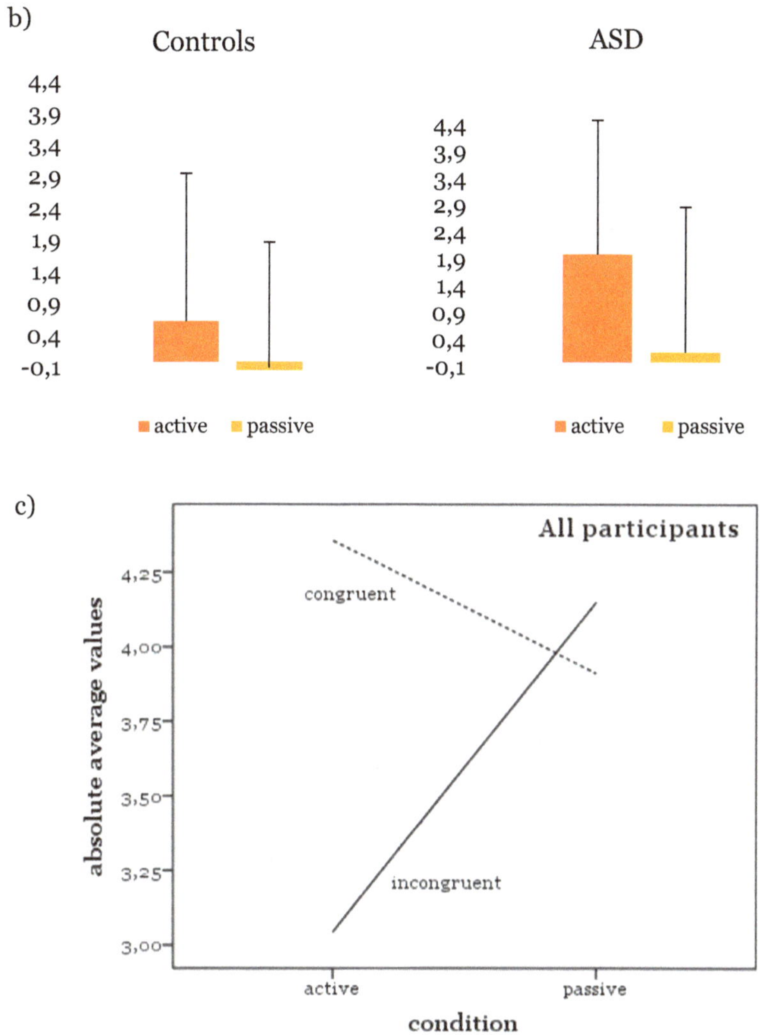

Figure 6 (continued). b) Plotted Emotional Egocentricity Bias for the conditions DOa and DOp separate for the two groups. c) Plotted condition x congruency interaction ($F(1,28) = 7.205$, $p = .012$, $\eta_p{}^2 = 0.205$). Source: Own depiction.

However, the participants in the ASD group shifted their empathic judgement more strongly towards their own emotional state (when the self and other were experiencing incongruent compared to congruent feelings) during this condition, showing a higher EEB than the control group, the latter demonstrating a lower EEB. During DOp, when the participants were passively observing a ball-game between four other players, both groups did not shift their empathic judgement in the direction their own emotional state, showing nearly no (and the controls even a negative) EEB (see Figure 5b). A four-factorial (2 x 2 x 2 x 2) mixed ANOVA (GLM) was calculated to assess differences in egocentric empathic judgements of both groups. The rating values related to exclusion of the other person were again inverted as in study 1 to ensure comparability of the EEBs regarding inclusion or exclusion of the other (see Figure 5a for the non-inverted values). A significant interaction for condition x congruency ($F_{(1,28)} = 7.205$, $p = .012$, $\eta_p^2 = 0.205$) could be observed (see Figure 5c). Planned comparisons via simple effects analysis revealed that this interaction was driven by a larger average difference between congruent and incongruent blocks in the DOa condition, where the participants were emotionally involved in the game (congruent – incongruent (M/SE) = 1.31/0.44; $p = .006$), than when the participants were merely observing the game (congruent – incongruent = -0.24/0.47; $p = .620$). In this context, it should again be noted that for DOa, the average judgements during congruent trials were higher than those during incongruent trials (congruent (M/SE) = 4.35/0.48; incongruent = 3.04/0.37), for DOp however, this difference was reversed (congruent (M/SE) = 3.91/0.53; incongruent = 4.15/0.44).

During emotional involvement, all 30 participants judged the opposite person in a significantly more egocentric way than during passive observation. However, no condition x congruency x group interaction could be found ($F_{(1,28)} = 0.220$, $p = .643$, $\eta_p^2 = 0.008$): Although planned comparisons indicated that participants with ASD judged the other person in a significantly more egocentric way during active emotional involvement (congruent – incongruent (M/SE) = 2.00/0.62; $p = .003$) in comparison to controls (congruent – incongruent (M/SE) = 0.62/0.62; $p = .321$), the three-way interaction with the factor group was not statistically significant, suggesting no differences between the controls and autistic subjects in this sample in regard to emotional egocentricity. In fact, the overall EEBs of the two groups were comparable in size and did not differ significantly in the active ($t_{(28)} = -1.555$, $p = .131$) nor the passive ($t_{(28)} = -0.868$, $p = .393$) condition.

Furthermore, there was a significant interaction for condition x valence x congruency ($F_{(1,28)}$ = 4.968, p = .034, η_p^2 = 0.151). Planned comparisons indicated that this interaction was driven by a significant difference between congruent and incongruent trials in the active condition during explicit exclusion of the other person (congruent – incongruent (*M/SE*) = 1.88; p = .003) in comparison to inclusion (congruent – incongruent = 0.75; p = .196). The participants showed a significant Inclusion Bias during first-hand emotional involvement independent of group, but no significant Exclusion Bias. All other main effects and interactions were not significant (see Table A6 in Appendix II).

To analyze separately whether the valence of the egocentric shift (in the positive or negative direction) was statistically different between the conditions, paired *t*-Tests were calculated separate for the two groups. The results indicated that the Inclusion and Exclusion Bias did not differ significantly from each other: This held true both for the control participants (active condition: $t(14)$ = 1.190, p = .254, Inclusion – Exclusion bias (*M/SE*) = 1.33/1.12; passive condition: ($t(14)$ = -1.059, p = .308, Inclusion – Exclusion bias (*M/SE*) = -1.02/0.96) and the participants with ASD (active condition: $t(14)$ = 0.984, p = .342, Inclusion – Exclusion bias (*M/SE*) = 0.93/0.95; passive condition: $t(14)$ = -0.407, p = .690, Inclusion – Exclusion bias (*M/SE*) = -0.35/0.86). In both conditions, the control and the ASD participants revealed similar shifts towards their own positive or negative emotional state when judging the other person.

In a second analysis step, the degree of alexithymia as well as the level of autistic traits were separately submitted into the ANOVA as covariates[6]. The results indicated a significant congruency x group interaction when controlling for alexithymia only ($F_{(1,27)}$ = 4.815, p = .037, η_p^2 = 0.151). Planned comparisons revealed that this interaction was driven by a significant difference between congruent and incongruent trials in the ASD group (congruent – incongruent (*M/SE*) = 1.568/0.59, p = .012) in contrast to the control group (congruent – incongruent (*M/SE*) = -0.493/0.59, p = .406). This group difference, however, was suppressed in

6 The covariates *alexithymia* and *autistic traits* were mean-centered before being put into the analysis by subtracting the mean from the value of each participant. This was done to ensure validity of the results of the mixed ANOVA (Delaney & Maxwell, 1981).

the main analysis and only emerged when entering alexithymia as a covariate. When keeping alexithymia levels constant, there was a significant group difference in the EEB independent of condition or valence. Moreover, there was still no 3-way interaction of condition x congruency x group ($F_{(1,27)} = 0.323$, $p = .574$, $\eta_p^2 = 0.012$), ruling out that any potential differences between controls and ASD participants in their egocentric judgements in the active versus the passive condition were masked by the level of alexithymia. All other main effects and interactions were not significant. Separately taking the degree of autistic traits into account lead to no significant changes in the main effects and interactions involving the between-subjects factor group (see Tables A7 and A8 in Appendix II for all main effects and interactions of the covariate analyses). In contrast to alexithymia, autistic traits had no suppressing effect on any group differences in this sample.

Table 6

Depression, trait empathy and alexithymia in the two groups.

Questionnaires	Controls	ASD	*t*	*df*	*p*
Depression (BDI)	6.20 (6.92)	12.93 (10.55)	-2.068	28	.048
Trait Empathy (IRI)					
Fantasy	3.04 (0.76)	2.49 (0.77)	1.941	28	.062
Empathic Concern	3.61 (0.74)	3.23 (0.75)	1.401	28	.172
Perspective Taking	3.67 (0.53)	2.99 (0.72)	2.952	28	.006
Personal Distress	2.46 (0.46)	3.00 (0.80)	-2.290	22.35	.032
Alexithymia (TAS)					
DIF	12.33 (4.85)	20.60 (5.96)	-4.166	28	< .001
DDF	12.27 (3.65)	18.40 (3.16)	-4.919	28	< .001
EOT	16.60 (4.07)	20.07 (4.38)	-2.214	28	.035
Sum of all Scales	41.20 (9.97)	58.29 (10.20)	-4.561	28	< .001

Note. Averages (standard deviations) as well as significance tests are given. DIF = Difficulty Identifying Feelings, DDF = Difficulty Describing Feelings, EOT = Externally Oriented Thinking.

Regarding the questionnaires, the two groups differed significantly in depressive symptoms, perspective taking and personal distress (see Table 6 for averages, standard deviations and significance tests). Autistic participants showed a higher degree of depressive symptoms, a lower ability for taking the perspective of another person and higher distress than control participants. They did not differ from controls in two scales assessing affective empathy (fantasy and empathic concern). However, autistic subjects had higher values in all subscales assessing alexithymia and differed significantly from controls in all of them.

To investigate associations of the mean EEBs and their difference in conditions of active emotional involvement and passive observation with alexithymia, trait empathy and autistic traits, two-sided Spearman correlations were calculated separate for the two groups. The difference between the active and passive EEB was not significantly associated with autistic traits or any of the scales assessing alexithymia and trait empathy in the control group. The results further indicated significant negative associations between the EEB in the active condition and empathic concern ($r_s = -.53$, $p = .041$), and (as in study 1) between the EEB in the passive condition and a difficulty to identify feelings ($r_s = -.67$, $p = .006$) in control subjects. Lower ability to show empathic concern for another person and less difficulty to identify feelings were both associated with a higher bias for participants in the control group. In the ASD group, only the scale measuring empathic concern was negatively associated with the difference between active and passive EEB ($r_s = -.53$, $p = .045$), with a lower ability to show empathic concern cohering with a higher difference. This again could have resulted either from a higher EEB in the active condition, a lower passive EEB or both. Furthermore, the passive EEB was significantly associated in a negative way with empathic concern ($r_s = -.56$, $p = .030$) and personal distress ($r_s = -.70$, $p = .004$). Lower ability to show empathic concern for another person and lower personal distress were both associated with a higher passive bias in participants with ASD (see Table A9 in Appendix II for all correlational results). Moreover, there were no significant correlations between autistic traits and any of the alexithymia scales in both groups (Controls: AQ & DIF, $r_s = .49$, $p = .064$; AQ & DDF, $r_s = .11$, $p = .703$; AQ & EOT, $r_s = .41$, $p = .127$; ASD: AQ & DIF, $r_s = .48$, $p = .069$; AQ & DDF, $r_s = .29$, $p = .300$; AQ & EOT, $r_s = .18$, $p = .531$). See Table A10 in Appendix II for results regarding the rating durations.

4.2 fMRI Results

In the following section, the neurophysiological results are presented. For all subsequent contrasts, no masking was applied, the uncorrected significance level was set at $p = .001$ and a cluster-extent based threshold of ≥ 10 significantly active voxels was applied[7]. For reasons of space, only the main effects and the interactions relevant for the hypotheses are presented separately for each study. Study 1 included 18 neurotypical male adults, study 2 consisted of 15 participants with ASD and 15 neurotypical controls.

4.2.1 Study 1

Effect of experiment. The main effect of the experiment primarily acted as a manipulation check to see if there was a difference on the neural level between completing the Cyberball task versus the baseline. A whole-brain contrast between the neural activity during watching the video vs. baseline revealed that participants displayed greater activity in the following areas during the game (*video > baseline*): Right middle temporal gyrus, bilateral calcarine cortex, left cuneus, left middle occipital gyrus and right fusiform gyrus (see Table 7).

Effect of emotional involvement. There were no significant suprathreshold clusters that showed enhanced hemodynamic activity in the active condition compared to the passive (*active > passive*), but there was enhanced activity in the following regions in the passive condition compared to the active condition (*passive > active*): Left middle frontal gyrus, vermis lobules IV and VI, right cerebellum crus I, bilateral cerebellum lobule VI, bilateral putamen, right amygdala, left posterior cingulate cortex, left insula, left precentral gyrus, right calcarine cortex, bilateral postcentral gyrus and left middle occipital gyrus (see Table 8 and Figure 6).

7 As Woo, Krishnan, and Wager (2014) reported, cluster-extent based thresholding increases the sensitivity in identifying significant regions, especially in moderate to small sample sizes ($n < 50$).

Table 7

Main effect of experiment (video > baseline).

Anatomical Region	H	cluster K	*T*	Z score	x, y, z
Middle temporal gyrus	R	1087	12.53	Inf	50, -70, 4
Calcarine cortex	R	1772	9.85	Inf	8, -94, 12
Calcarine cortex	L		9.84	Inf	-2, -98, 4
Cuneus	L		9.29	Inf	-10, -92, 16
Middle occipital gyrus	L	756	8.86	7.84	-46, -72, 4
Fusiform gyrus	R	42	4.21	4.07	42, -40, -16

Note. H = hemisphere. Coordinates are given in mm.

Effect of social pain. Focusing on the valence comparison over both conditions and congruency levels, the right middle temporal gyrus and the right fusiform gyrus were activated to a greater extent during another's inclusion than during exclusion (*inclusion > exclusion*; see Table A4 in Appendix I). For the opposite contrast (*exclusion > inclusion*), enhanced activations during exclusion of another person were found in the following regions: Right precentral gyrus, bilateral postcentral gyrus, left calcarine cortex, left cuneus, left superior occipital gyrus, bilateral superior medial frontal gyrus, left medial cingulate cortex, right supplementary motor area, right insula and right superior temporal pole (see Table 9 and Figure 7).

Table 8
Main effect of condition (passive > active).

Anatomical Region	H	cluster K	*T*	Z score	x, y, z
Middle frontal gyrus	L	229	4.84	4.64	-32, 32, 28
Vermis lobule VI	L	353	4.71	4.53	-2, -66, -8
Vermis lobule IV	L		4.15	4.02	-2, -58, 0
Cerebellum crus I	R		3.65	3.55	42, -58, -38
Cerebellum lobule VI	L	188	3.98	3.87	-24, -50, -28
Cerebellum lobule VI	L		3.36	3.29	-22, -62, -20
Cerebellum lobule VI	R	227	3.66	3.57	18, -60, -20
Cerebellum lobule VI	R		3.50	3.42	22, -66, -28
Putamen	R	46	4.28	4.14	30, 2, 2
Putamen	L	162	4.04	3.92	-26, 8, 12
Putamen	L		3.58	3.50	-28, -2, 14
Amygdala	R		4.16	4.03	30, -4, -14
Posterior cingulate cortex	L	99	4.22	4.08	-10, -40, 18
Insula	L		3.78	3.68	-28, 12, -12
Precentral gyrus	L	37	3.57	3.49	-48, 2, 32
Calcarine cortex	R	24	3.56	3.47	18, -86, 0
Postcentral gyrus	L	38	3.53	3.44	-36, -28, 42
Postcentral gyrus	R	13	3.31	3.24	38, -34, 54
Middle occipital gyrus	L	21	3.31	3.24	-26, -68, 38

Note. H = hemisphere. Coordinates are given in mm.

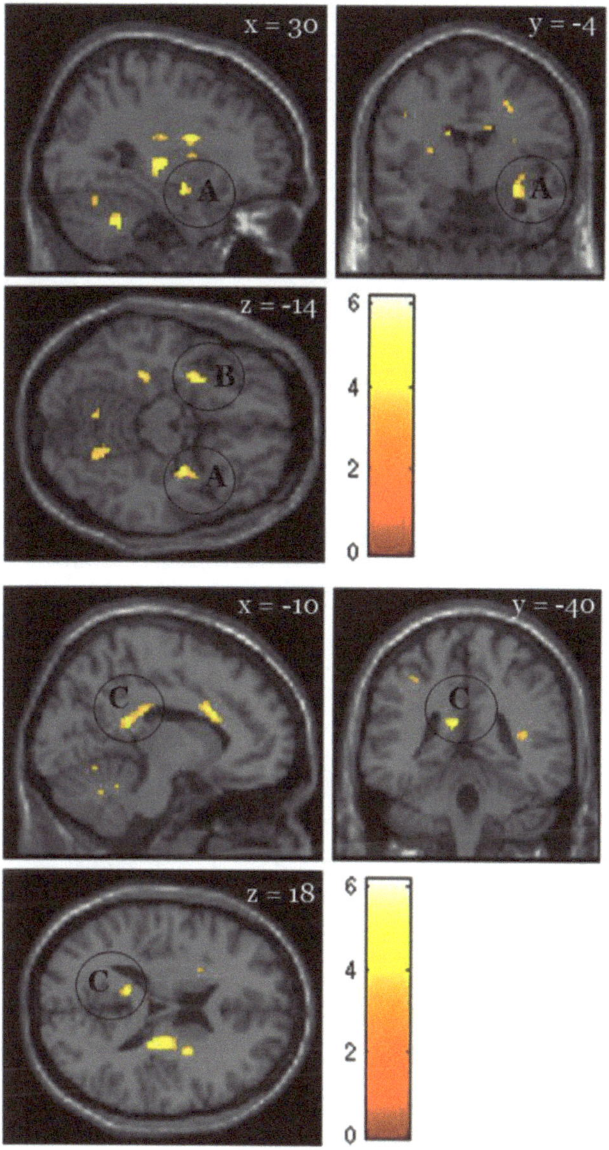

Figure 6. Enhanced activations for the main effect of condition (*passive* > *active*) were i.a. found in right amygdala (A), left insula (B) and left posterior cingulate cortex (C). The sample size was n_1 = 18. Source: Own depiction.

Table 9
Main effect of valence (Other exclusion > Other inclusion).

Anatomical Region	H	cluster K	*T*	Z score	x, y, z
Precentral gyrus	R	434	5.21	4.97	22, -22, 68
Postcentral gyrus	R		4.75	4.56	24, -36, 66
Postcentral gyrus	L	451	4.41	4.26	-20, -32, 68
Calcarine cortex	L	1508	5.21	4.96	-4, -90, -6
Calcarine cortex	L		5.02	4.80	2, -82, -4
Cuneus	L	112	3.92	3.81	-4, -84, 36
Superior occipital gyrus	L		3.21	3.15	-18, -88, 40
Superior medial frontal gyrus	L	113	3.89	3.78	-10, 50, 44
Superior medial frontal gyrus	L	11	3.29	3.23	0, 48, 46
Superior medial frontal gyrus	R	65	3.64	3.55	6, 60, 38
Superior medial frontal gyrus	R		3.39	3.31	12, 56, 42
Medial cingulate cortex	L	164	3.71	3.61	0, -22, 46
Supplementary motor area	R		3.57	3.49	0, -16, 64
Insula	R	31	3.51	3.42	46, 6, -6
Superior temporal pole	R		3.35	3.28	52, 12, -12

Note. H = hemisphere. Coordinates are given in mm.

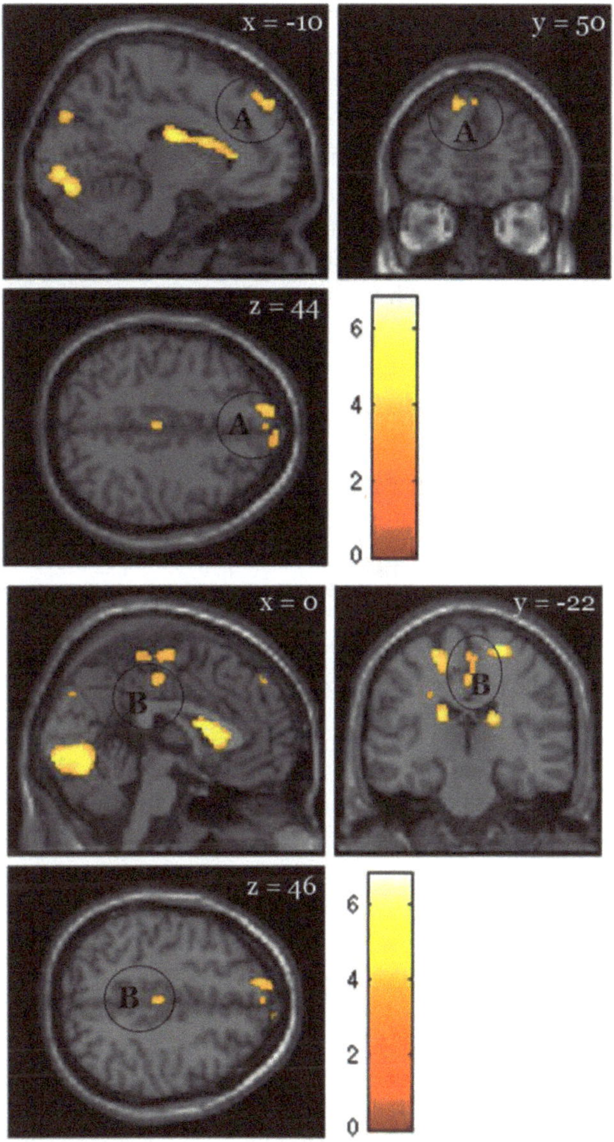

Figure 7. Enhanced activations for the main effect of social pain (*exclusion* > *inclusion*) were i.a. found in bilateral dorsolateral prefrontal (A) and left medial cingulate (B) cortices. The sample size was n_1 = 18. Source: Own depiction.

Effect of emotional egocentricity. To investigate the occurrence of an EEB independent of condition or valence, the difference in neurophysiological activation between congruent and incongruent trials was evaluated. The first contrast (*congruent > incongruent*) revealed enhanced activity in the bilateral putamen, left lingual gyrus and right calcarine cortex, when the self and other were experiencing similar emotional states compared to when they were not (see Table A5 in Appendix I). For the opposite contrast (*incongruent > congruent*), the following areas showed greater activity, when conversing feelings of the self and other had to be distinguished: Bilateral precuneus, bilateral middle temporal gyrus, bilateral superior parietal gyrus, bilateral postcentral gyrus and right lingual gyrus (see Table 10).

Table 10
Main effect of congruency (incongruent > congruent).

Anatomical Region	H	cluster K	*T*	Z score	x, y, z
Precuneus	L	731	4.70	4.52	-6, -46, 60
Precuneus	R		4.12	3.99	10, -46, 66
Middle temporal gyrus	L	77	3.96	3.85	-56, -42, 12
Middle temporal gyrus	R	20	3.51	3.43	48, -64, 8
Superior parietal gyrus	L	64	3.88	3.77	-30, -50, 64
Superior parietal gyrus	R	63	3.65	3.56	44, -40, 60
Postcentral gyrus	L		3.65	3.56	-34, -42, 66
Postcentral gyrus	R	54	3.47	3.39	30, -44, 64
Postcentral gyrus	R		3.31	3.24	30, -36, 66
Lingual gyrus	R	43	3.84	3.73	12, -86, -14

Note. H = hemisphere. Coordinates are given in mm.

Interaction effect of condition and congruency. Since the behavioral data showed a significant bias in the active condition in contrast to the passive condition, it was also investigated in the fMRI data: The contrast comparing the difference in congruency (*active (incongruent > congruent) > passive (incongruent > congruent))* in the active to the passive condition revealed no significant suprathreshold clusters. However, in the active condition, the following areas were significantly more active during congruent in contrast to incongruent trials (*active (congruent > incongruent) > passive (congruent > incongruent))*: Left superior temporal gyrus, left supramarginal gyrus, right middle frontal gyrus, right paracentral lobule, bilateral medial cingulate cortex and left inferior parietal lobule (see Table 11 and Figure 8).

Table 11
Interaction effect of condition x congruency: Active (congruent > incongruent) > Passive (congruent > incongruent).

Anatomical Region	H	cluster K	*T*	Z score	x, y, z
Superior temporal gyrus	L	239	3.98	3.86	-54, -34, 24
Supramarginal gyrus	L		3.93	3.82	-66, -34, 24
Supramarginal gyrus	L		3.36	3.29	-66, -22, 26
Middle frontal gyrus	R	39	3.56	3.47	30, 32, 46
Paracentral lobule	R	39	3.46	3.38	10, -24, 62
Medial cingulate cortex	R	30	3.44	3.36	10, -14, 34
Medial cingulate cortex	R	28	3.43	3.35	8, -22, 44
Medial cingulate cortex	L	17	3.43	3.35	-10, -10, 40
Inferior parietal lobule	L	20	3.33	3.26	-34, -36, 44

Note. H = hemisphere. Coordinates are given in mm.

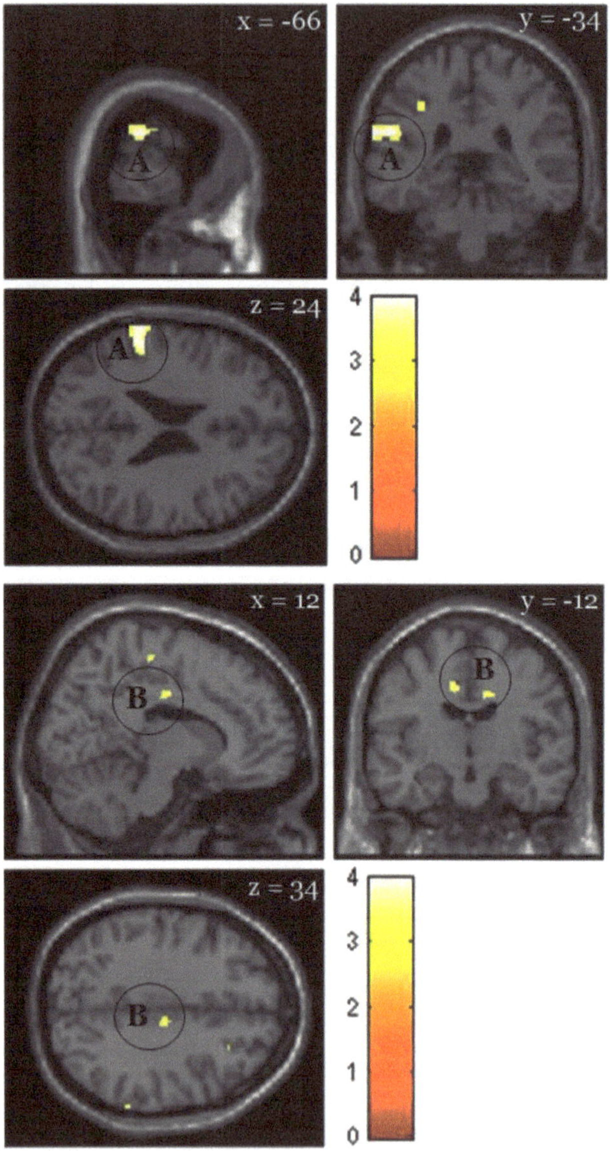

Figure 8. Enhanced activations for the interaction effect condition x congruency (*Active: congruent > incongruent > Passive: congruent > incongruent*) were i.a. found in left supramarginal gyrus (A) and bilateral medial cingulate cortices (B). The sample size was n_1 = 18. Source: Own depiction.

4.2.2 Study 2

Effect of experiment. The whole-brain contrast between the neural activity during watching the video vs. baseline revealed that all participants displayed greater activity in the following areas during the game: Right middle temporal gyrus, left middle occipital gyrus, bilateral calcarine cortex, left lingual gyrus, right fusiform gyrus and right superior temporal gyrus (see Table 12).

Table 12
Main effect of experiment (video > baseline).

Anatomical Region	H	cluster K	*T*	Z score	x, y, z
Middle temporal gyrus	R	1360	14.06	Inf	50, -72, 0
Middle temporal gyrus	R		13.69	Inf	50, -64, 4
Middle occipital gyrus	L	952	13.38	Inf	-46, -72, 6
Calcarine cortex	L	1893	13.02	Inf	-6, -94, 10
Calcarine cortex	R		11.28	Inf	10, -92, 14
Lingual gyrus	L		3.94	3.87	-12, -74, -8
Fusiform gyrus	R	25	4.13	4.05	42, -40, -18
Superior temporal gyrus	R	11	3.53	3.48	50, -38, 12

Note. H = hemisphere. Coordinates are given in mm.

Effect of group. Looking at the overall differences between the two groups independent of condition, valence and congruency, the group contrast favoring control participants (*control > ASD*) showed no significant suprathreshold clusters. However, the opposite contrast (*ASD > control*) revealed greater activity in the following regions in the ASD group: Left superior frontal gyrus, bilateral calcarine cortex, bilateral lingual gyrus, left middle occipital gyrus, left cerebellum lobule VI and right Heschl gyrus (see Table 13).

Table 13
Main effect of group (ASD > control).

Anatomical Region	H	cluster K	*T*	Z score	x, y, z
Superior frontal gyrus	L	339	4.44	4.34	-18, -58, 8
Calcarine cortex	L		4.29	4.20	-12, -64, 18
Calcarine cortex	R	202	4.31	4.22	18, -54, 8
Calcarine cortex	L	37	3.54	3.49	-4, -94, 6
Calcarine cortex	L		3.33	3.29	4, -92, 4
Lingual gyrus	L		3.48	3.43	-16, -44, 0
Lingual gyrus	R	65	3.80	3.74	20, -66, -8
Lingual gyrus	R	20	3.45	3.40	6, -66, 6
Middle occipital gyrus	L	63	3.91	3.84	-40, -74, 2
Cerebellum lobule VI	L	26	3.70	3.64	-16, -60, -14
Heschl gyrus	R		3.24	3.20	40, -22, 2

Note. H = hemisphere. Coordinates are given in mm.

Effect of emotional involvement. Regarding the two different conditions of Cyberball, the main effect contrasts revealed greater activity in the active compared to the passive (*active > passive*) in the left cuneus (cluster K = 161, *T* = 4.27, Z = 4.18, coordinates (x, y, z) = -6, -92, 16). However, the contrast favoring the condition, where the participants were merely observing others play (*passive > active*) revealed no enhanced activations.

Effect of social pain. Focusing on the valence comparison between trials of inclusion and exclusion over both groups, conditions and congruency levels, the following regions were activated to a greater extent during inclusion than during exclusion (*inclusion > exclusion*): Right inferior occipital gyrus, right superior temporal gyrus, left fusiform gyrus and right middle temporal gyrus (see Table A11 in Appendix II). For the opposite contrast (*exclusion > inclusion*), no enhanced activated voxels could be detected, when the other person was excluded during Cyberball.

Effect of emotional egocentricity. To investigate the occurrence of an EEB independent of group, condition or valence, the difference between congruent and incongruent trials was evaluated. The first contrast (*congruent > incongruent*) revealed enhanced activation in the right calcarine cortex (cluster K = 25, *T* = 3.74, Z = 3.68, coordinates (x, y, z) = 20, -50, 6), when the self and the other person were experiencing similar emotional states compared to when they were not. For the opposite contrast (*incongruent > congruent*), the following areas showed greater activity, when conversing feelings of the self and other had to be distinguished: Right caudate nucleus, left superior medial frontal gyrus, right lingual gyrus, bilateral cerebellum crus I, bilateral middle frontal gyrus, bilateral superior frontal gyrus, right superior temporal gyrus, bilateral middle temporal gyrus, right precentral gyrus, bilateral precuneus, right superior parietal gyrus, bilateral postcentral gyrus, left inferior parietal lobule, right inferior temporal gyrus, left inferior orbitofrontal gyrus, vermis lobule IV, left cerebellum lobules IV/V, left angular gyrus and left middle occipital gyrus (see Table 14).

Table 14
Main effect of congruency (incongruent > congruent).

Anatomical Region	H	cluster K	*T*	Z score	x, y, z
Caudate nucleus	R		4.79	4.67	6, 20, 6
Superior medial frontal gyrus	L	1718	4.84	4.71	-10, 32, 60
Superior medial frontal gyrus	L		4.80	4.68	0, 46, 46
Superior medial frontal gyrus	L		4.68	4.56	0, 38, 56
Lingual gyrus	R	1027	4.27	4.18	12, -88, -10
Cerebellum crus I	L		3.98	3.91	-16, -78, -20

(continued)

Table 14
Main effect of congruency (incongruent > congruent) (continued).

Anatomical Region	H	cluster K	*T*	Z score	x, y, z
Cerebellum crus I	R		3.46	3.41	24, -76, -30
Cerebellum crus I	R		3.35	3.31	30, -78, -24
Middle frontal gyrus	L	238	4.13	4.05	-42, 26, 46
Middle frontal gyrus	L		3.31	3.27	-36, 16, 58
Middle frontal gyrus	R	26	3.36	3.32	50, 26, 44
Middle frontal gyrus	R		3.25	3.21	52, 28, 36
Middle frontal gyrus	L	11	3.28	3.24	-24, 24, 58
Middle frontal gyrus	R	14	3.27	3.23	34, 2, 64
Superior frontal gyrus	L		3.82	3.76	-24, 8, 68
Superior frontal gyrus	R	20	3.45	3.41	24, 6, 68
Superior temporal gyrus	R	131	4.13	4.05	50, -36, 10
Middle temporal gyrus	R		3.80	3.73	64, -40, 12
Middle temporal gyrus	L	52	3.91	3.84	-56, -8, -14
Middle temporal gyrus	L		3.39	3.34	-50, -12, -10
Middle temporal gyrus	L	42	3.42	3.37	-54, -66, 16
Middle temporal gyrus	L		3.30	3.25	-44, -64, 10
Precentral gyrus	R		3.71	3.65	24, -30, 68
Precentral gyrus	R	49	3.43	3.39	52, 10, 46

(continued)

Table 14
Main effect of congruency (incongruent > congruent) (continued).

Anatomical Region	H	cluster K	*T*	Z score	x, y, z
Precentral gyrus	R		3.18	3.14	44, 4, 48
Precuneus	R		3.69	3.63	4, -48, 54
Precuneus	L	103	3.82	3.75	-6, -36, 60
Superior parietal gyrus	R	270	3.96	3.89	32, -44, 60
Postcentral gyrus	R		3.41	3.36	36, -32, 54
Postcentral gyrus	L	23	3.36	3.32	-26, -32, 58
Inferior parietal lobule	L	66	3.76	3.69	-34, -42, 52
Inferior temporal gyrus	R	153	3.75	3.69	52, -72, -2
Inferior orbitofrontal gyrus	L	28	3.59	3.54	-40, 22, -14
Vermis lobule IV	R	106	3.59	3.54	2, -52, -6
Vermis lobule IV	R		3.47	3.42	4, -60, -10
Cerebellum lobules IV/V	L		3.40	3.35	-4, -42, -8
Angular gyrus	L	75	3.56	3.50	-42, -68, 30
Middle occipital gyrus	L	30	3.56	3.50	-42, -80, -16

Note. H = hemisphere. Coordinates are given in mm.

Furthermore, since study 1 generated little activation during incongruent trials in controls, the main effect of the EEB was investigated separately only for autistic subjects: Enhanced hemodynamic activity was found in right caudate nucleus, left superior medial frontal gyrus, left superior and middle frontal gyri, left inferior orbitofrontal cortex, left cerebellum crus I, left cerebellum lobule VI, right vermis lobules IV and V, right cuneus, right calcarine cortex, left middle temporal gyrus, bilateral postcentral gyrus, left paracentral lobule, right hippocampus, left angular gyrus and right precentral gyrus during incongruent compared to congruent (*ASD incongruent > ASD congruent*) trials (see Table 15 and Figure 9).

Table 15
Main effect of congruency (ASD incongruent > ASD congruent).

Anatomical Region	H	cluster K	*T*	Z score	x, y, z
Caudate nucleus	R	1571	4.25	4.16	6, 18, 6
Superior medial frontal gyrus	L	456	4.16	4.08	-10, 34, 62
Superior medial frontal gyrus			3.72	3.66	0, 48, 48
Superior medial frontal gyrus		73	3.62	3.56	0, 56, 32
Superior frontal gyrus	L		3.68	3.62	-20, 50, 42
Middle frontal gyrus	L	11	3.27	3.22	-42, 24, 44
Inferior orbitofrontal cortex	L	35	3.93	3.86	-38, 24, -14
Cerebellum crus I	L	417	3.82	3.75	-8, -78, -18
Cerebellum lobule VI	L	58	3.38	3.34	-4, -62, -14
Vermis lobules IV/V	R		3.30	3.26	4, -60, -10
Cuneus	R		3.52	3.47	4, .74, -24
Calcarine cortex	R		3.50	3.45	2, -80, -8
Middle temporal gyrus	L	30	3.54	3.49	-50, -12, -10
Caudate nucleus	R	1571	4.25	4.16	6, 18, 6

(continued)

Table 15
Main effect of congruency (ASD incongruent > ASD congruent) (continued).

Anatomical Region	H	cluster K	*T*	Z score	x, y, z
Postcentral gyrus	R	47	3.49	3.44	26, -32, 68
Postcentral gyrus	L	76	3.37	3.33	-24, -30, 68
Postcentral gyrus	L		3.33	3.29	-24, -32, 58
Paracentral lobule	L	68	3.46	3.41	-6, -34, 62
Hippocampus	R	28	3.40	3.36	38, -22, -10
Angular gyrus	L	15	3.31	3.27	-40, -66, 30
Precentral gyrus	R	17	3.20	3.16	32, -6, 48

Note. H = hemisphere. Coordinates are given in mm.

Interaction effects of group, condition and congruency. Since the behavioral analysis revealed a significant interaction for condition x congruency for study 2, this was further investigated in the fMRI data. However, the contrasts regarding the congruency difference between the active and the passive condition (*active (congruent > incongruent) > passive (congruent > incongruent)* and *active (incongruent > congruent) > passive (incongruent > congruent))* both revealed no significant suprathreshold clusters. Although the three-way interaction was not significant in the behavioral results, it was investigated in the fMRI data due to the prior hypotheses. However, there were no significant suprathreshold clusters for any of the contrasts.

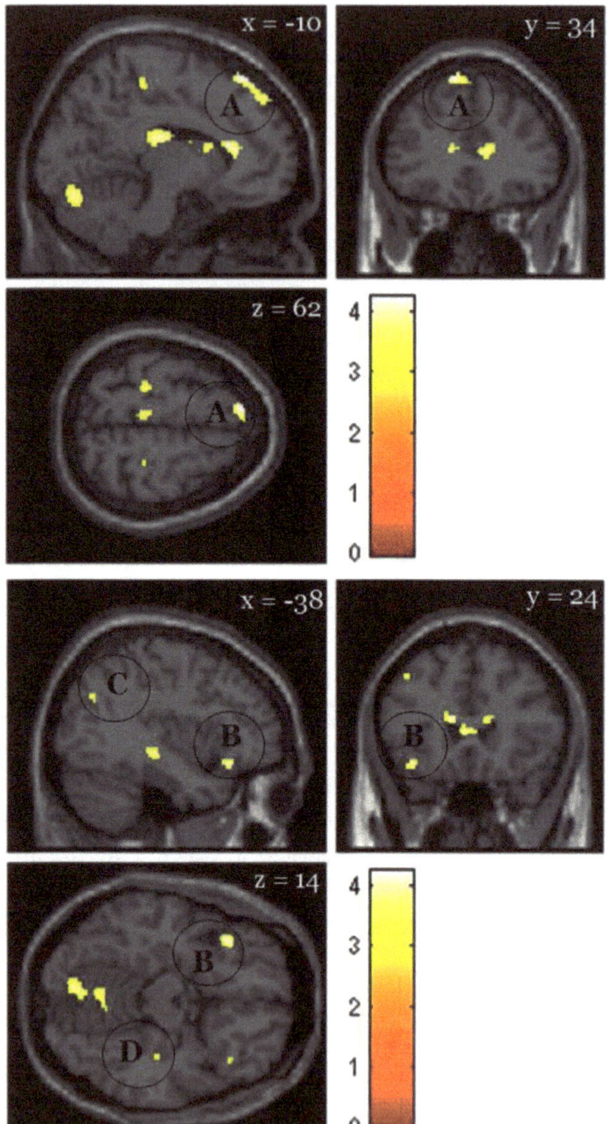

Figure 9. Enhanced activations for the main effect of congruency (*incongruent* > *congruent*) only for the autistic subjects ($n_1 = 15$) were i.a. found in left dorsolateral prefrontal cortex (A), left orbitofrontal gyrus (B), left angular gyrus (C) and right hippocampus (D). Source: Own depiction.

5 Discussion

Empathy and its distinct affective and cognitive components have been widely studied in both neurotypical as well as specific psychiatric populations (Decety, 2015; Lamm et al., 2016). Several previous studies have shown that the cognitive component of empathy – encompassing concepts like perspective taking, mentalizing and theory of mind – seems to be qualitatively different, or even disrupted, in Autism-Spectrum-Disorder (ASD; Bird & Viding, 2014; Lockwood, 2016; Lockwood et al., 2013). In this context, the ability for self-other distinction (SOD) plays a crucial role in empathic processing, mainly to avoid personal distress and confusion, when one is confronted with various and changing emotional states of other people that do not necessarily always match one's own. But human social cognition skills are not totally free from error: Since we primarily use our own emotions and perceptions in guiding our thoughts about others in the environment, such a self-projection mechanism can lead to empathic judgements that are egocentrically biased towards the self-perspective (Hoffmann et al., 2016; Silani et al., 2013; Steinbeis & Singer, 2014). Because of their problems regarding the cognitive domain of empathy, autistic individuals might have considerably more difficulties in recognizing and distinguishing feelings of themselves and other individuals.

The recruitment of processes related to SOD and the occurrence of the emotional egocentricity bias (EEB) was investigated in two subsequent studies, both assessing behavioral as well as neuroimaging data via fMRI. First, a sample of neurotypical adult participants without psychiatric or neurological disorders was explored regarding the general occurrence of egocentric judgements. Secondly, an experimental group of participants with Asperger syndrome was matched with neurotypical controls from the first sample to investigate intergroup differences. The present thesis used an adapted version of the well-known Cyberball paradigm (Novembre et al., 2015; Williams et al., 2000) to measure (short-term) empathy for social exclusion as well as to assess differences in SOD and the emotional egocentricity bias during congruent and incongruent feeling states by means of manipulating the emotional involvement of the participants (playing versus observing).

Many studies have shown that people with ASD show decreased attention to the face and eye region (Blair, Frith, Smith, Abell, & Cipolotti, 2002;

H. Hartmann, *Social Interactions in Autism*, BestMasters,
https://doi.org/10.1007/978-3-658-22013-6_5

Klin, Jones, Schultz, Volkmar, & Cohen, 2002) and might have problems in tasks that require the perception and processing of emotional facial expressions (Johnstone, Kim, & Whalen, 2009; Mazza et al., 2014). Therefore, the present paradigm avoided the recognition of facial cues to overcome these methodological issues related to assessing empathy by using facial expressions in ASD but still aimed at recreating a realistic social setting. In fact, positive and negative emotional states of the other person had to be mentally inferred by the participants. The paradigm therefore controlled for the fact that any empathic abilities and emotional responses that the participants reported were due to poor facial emotion recognition skills.

Healthy adults behaviorally exhibited a significant EEB when they were actively playing, i.e. emotionally involved in the ball-game, confirming our prior hypothesis. When experiencing incongruent emotional states, the participants judged the other person's feelings in a more egocentric way in comparison to when in a congruent state. As shown by a direct statistical comparison, the EEB was of a similar size for biased judgements in the direction of the participant's own positive (Inclusion Bias) or negative state (Exclusion Bias) in both studies, showing that emotional egocentricity occurred equally intensive in both valence directions. This result might be an indication that first-hand feelings of inclusion were able to bias empathic judgements of another person just as much as feelings of exclusion and vice versa. When the participants were passively observing four others play the game, i.e. not directly emotionally involved, the difference between incongruent and congruent trials was not significant and no EEB was observed. This confirms our hypothesis that the recruitment of SOD to overcome an egocentric perspective was only needed in situations of direct emotional involvement and not during mere observation. These results are also in line with previous studies that found a significant EEB using different paradigms for the induction of pleasant and unpleasant emotions, e.g. affective touch or envy as well as similar sizes of biased judgement for positive and negative emotions (Riva et al., 2016; Silani et al., 2013; Steinbeis et al., 2015; Steinbeis & Singer, 2014). On a behavioral level, the here deployed version of Cyberball seemed to produce strong feelings of social inclusion/exclusion and was as able to generate an overall EEB for social pain to a similar extent compared with other paradigms. This suggests that emotional egocentricity might be a general concept evoked in many different emotional situations. The fact that no bias was found in the passive condition reliably ruled out that the participants were using 2nd order Theory of Mind (ToM) processes to guide their empathic judgements (e.g. having thoughts about other people's mental states: "The included opposite player sees another player getting excluded from the game, so he must feel bad for that person and therefore also feel the same way that person does"). If this would have been the case, a significant EEB would also have been observed in the passive condition. However, in contrast to the active condition, no emotional involvement (and therefore no active change of one's own neutral emotional state) lead to no difficulties in accurately judging another person's emotions. This might point to the conclusion that during mere observation of another's emotional state, the differentiation between self- and other-related states is not required as strongly as during active involvement. This is an important new insight that had not been investigated before and will add to preexisting knowledge about the specific context-dependent recruitment of SOD processes.

Interestingly, the intensities of empathic judgements for congruent and incongruent emotional states were reversed in the active and passive condition in both studies. For the calculation of the EEB, this doesn't seem relevant at first sight, because the level of egocentricity is defined as the difference between the two congruency conditions. However, the reversed averages should also be discussed in relation to the EEB: During congruent active emotional involvement, participants rated the other person as feeling more intense (independent of the valence) in contrast to incongruent trials. This seems logical, since an incongruence of self- and other-related emotional states is accompanied by greater difficulty to entangle those emotions and correctly tag feelings of the self and other. One reason why participants assigned less intense feeling states to the other person in those situations could therefore be the fact that they were simultaneously biased by their own feelings. This effect was reversed in the passive condition, where participants assigned stronger feelings of exclusion or inclusion during incongruent situations. However, the difference between congruent and incongruent trials in the passive condition was very small and not significant, indicating rather similar judgement intensities for both trials. This further supports our hypothesis that individuals are correctly able to judge another's emotional state, when they are not emotionally involved, and that this effect does not depend on whether the other person is experiencing similar or different emotions.

The second sample in study 2, including both participants with Asperger syndrome and mainly neurotypical controls from the first study, revealed a similarly strong EEB as in study 1: During emotional involvement, all participants judged the opposite person in a significantly more egocentric way than during passive observation, as indicated by a significant condition x congruency interaction. Considering the separate average ratings in the two groups, it should be noted, that this interaction was now mainly driven by the empathic ratings of the ASD participants, who showed a very strong EEB in the active condition. The control group on its own showed nearly no emotional egocentricity in both conditions. This rather surprising difference between the control participants of the two studies could, however, have been due to the reduction of the sample size for matching purposes: In the first sample with 20 participants, an EEB was clearly observed, but when reducing the control sample to 15 for the group comparison with the ASD group, the EEB disappeared (see also below for other limitations regarding the sample size).

However, there were no differences in the overall EEBs between the two groups, suggesting similar abilities of SOD and, in turn, equivalent skills for overcoming egocentricity in this sample. These results were fortified by the fact that the separate Inclusion and Exclusion Biases of the two groups were of a comparable size and did not differ significantly from each other. This is contrary to our prior hypothesis, which assumed ASD participants to exhibit stronger egocentric judgements because of an impaired ability to distinguish self- and other-related states. Although this was clearly indicated on a descriptive level by the averages in each group, the difference between the group EEBs was not statistically significant. Emotional egocentricity in both individuals with ASD and healthy controls, but no differences in emotional egocentricity between the groups, was also recently reported by Hoffmann et al. (2016) in a much larger sample. The authors only found deficits in autistic participants regarding ToM, but relatively intact SOD. This might indicate that self-other differentiation in autistic individuals could in fact function to an extent that is comparable to neurotypical individuals. In line with this, participants with ASD in this study were found to show a significantly lower ability for taking the perspective of another person than control participants. This cognitive empathic ability was not associated with any of the EEB scores in both groups. However, since the current study did not investigate ToM abilities using a behavioral task in comparison to SOD, future studies are needed to disentangle the impairments in autism related to cognitive empathy, self-other-distinction and mentalizing. On the other hand, the EEB significantly correlated with measures of affective empathy, including empathic concern and personal distress, and thus pointing to a negative connection between affective empathic processing and emotional egocentricity. Furthermore, autistic traits were not significantly correlated with the active or passive EEB. Since many authors have found intact affective empathy in autism (Bird et al., 2010; Dziobek et al., 2008; Rogers et al., 2007), this might explain why autistic participants did not show significant impairments in egocentricity: The elicited empathic feelings of social exclusion by means of Cyberball could have been processed more with the affective than the cognitive component or equally with both. Studies targeting this issue in the future should therefore focus on entangling measures of cognitive and affective empathy during Cyberball and clearing up the distinction between affective versus cognitive parts of SOD (for reviews on the matter see Lamm et al., 2016 and Steinbeis, 2016).

Controlling for the degree of autistic traits did not have any effect, suggesting that it did not mask any underlying group differences. Interestingly, when entering alexithymia as a covariate into the model, a previously not observed group difference regarding the factor congruency was found. The results showed that participants with ASD now displayed a significant EEB in contrast to controls independent of condition or valence. However, there was still no group difference between the two conditions active and passive. In our sample, alexithymia could have worked as a pulling force that in a way inhibited emotional egocentricity, letting a higher EEB in individuals with ASD only show, when the level of alexithymia was kept constant. Indeed, there was a significant difference between the groups in their alexithymic traits in which autistic individuals described themselves as more alexithymic. This might suggest that alexithymia executed a rather strong effect on any of the results regarding the ASD group and therefore could have led to the prior suppression of group differences in the intensity of the EEB by means of alexithymia. In fact, these results were further underlined by the negative association of the EEB in the passive condition and a difficulty to identify feelings – a primary symptom of alexithymia. In both studies, control participants who had greater difficulties to identify feelings exhibited a lower bias in the passive condition. This continues to suggest that low alexithymia, accompanied by a higher ability to identify and describe emotional states of oneself and of others, is associated with increased egocentricity. Highly alexithymic individuals, on the other hand, may not be confronted as much with possibly confusing, incongruent feelings of the self and other due to the nature of their condition. As a result, they might show less of a bias. However, because the present study only found an association of alexithymia with the bias in the passive condition and only for the control participants, this idea should be regarded as purely hypothetical for now and carefully investigated in future studies, assessing the EEB in groups of typically developing and autistic individuals with both high and low alexithymic traits.

On the neurophysiological level, the results of the two studies were rather inconclusive compared to the reported behavioral data. In both studies, the main effect of the experiment showed enhanced activations in the visual cortex and in regions associated with the visuospatial perception of human movement and facial stimuli (Grossman & Blake, 2002; Servos, Osu, Santi, & Kawato, 2002) as well as spatial attention (Martínez et al., 1999). These activations are in line with the fact that the participants were watching white silhouettes of moving figures playing a ball-game compared to the baseline.

However, the results regarding the other main effects and interactions differed strongly between the two studies: Comparing the two conditions (active emotional involvement vs. passive observation) with each other, enhanced hemodynamic activity was found in the passive condition in regions associated with working memory and executive functioning (Rajah, Languay, & Grady, 2011), language processing and reading (Booth, Wood, Lu, Houk, & Bitan, 2007; Oberhuber et al., 2013), somatosensory-related hand and finger movements (Yousry et al., 1997), memory, as well as the first-hand and empathic processing of positive and negative emotional stimuli (Maddock, 1999; Rütgen et al., 2015; Singer et al., 2004; Woo et al., 2014). For the latter, those were activated voxels in the right amygdala, left PCC and left insula. Apart from those, the previously mentioned regions coding for movement, spatial orientation and vision were also enhanced during passive observation. This was only observed in study 1, while study 2 generated no such activations. Interestingly, activations in the amygdala, cingulate cortex and insula have mainly been associated with the affective-motivational component of first-hand pain processing (Tracey & Mantyh, 2007) as well as the affective component of empathy (Shamay-Tsoory, 2011; Walter, 2012), lending further support to the notion that this version of Cyberball may in fact not only recruit cognitive empathic processes, but elicit a substantial affective neural response to emotional stimuli. Although SOD is primarily defined as a cognitive process, social exclusion is a type of "pain" that has been shown to elicit very strong emotional reactions (Eisenberger, 2011, 2012). For example, as Novembre et al. (2015) was recently able to show with very a similar version of Cyberball, that areas coding for the affective-motivational component of physical pain (e.g. ACC, posterior insula) were not only activated during first-hand social rejection but also during empathy for someone that was being excluded. One explanation, why these regions were increasingly enhanced in the passive condition, might be the fact that the participants were able to focus completely on judging the feelings of the other person. In the active condition, however, they were additionally required to keep track of their own feelings at the same time, which might have decreased their empathic response and led to a lack of increased activation in regions associated with empathy. Unexpectedly, there were no other enhanced activations in the active condition compared to the passive (besides in regions of vision and motion in study 2). Since the participants were pressing buttons, throwing the ball and actively playing, enhanced activations in areas of motor activity were predicted in this condition, but this was not found in our sample. One reason for the lack of differences regarding motor activity in the two conditions could be the fact that the length of the blocks was too long, leading to a decrease of overall signal and a subsequent loss of enhanced activation over time.

Focusing on the main effect of social pain, exclusion of another person activated left MCC and right insula to a greater extent than during inclusion. As mentioned before, a network including the dorsal ACC, MCC and AI has repeatedly been associated with arousal, the processing of aversive affective states and pain unpleasantness in general, and has also been found in studies specifically targeting social rejection (Eisenberger, 2015; Eisenberger et al., 2003; Lamm, Decety, & Singer, 2011). This converges with the behavioral ratings of the participants, who judged the other as feeling more negative during exclusion and more positive during inclusion. Furthermore, bilateral dorsolateral prefrontal cortices (dlPFC) and the right superior TP were enhanced during exclusion, regions often associated with ToM, perspective taking and mentalizing about other's as well as one's own mental states (Singer, 2006; van Veluw & Chance, 2014). Interestingly, those regions were not activated during inclusion trials, possibly because the focus of the Cyberball game tends to be negatively-valenced (although equal amounts and combinations of both positive and negative emotions were induced). However, it might be that Cyberball was not as able as expected to produce strong positive reactions, but simply achieve variations on a scale from positively neutral to negative. This stronger deviation from the default neutral emotional state into the negative direction might be one explanation why stronger activity in regions coding for perspective taking were needed during exclusion of another person. On the other hand, empathic judgements about neutral to positive states could have been more intuitive and therefore easier to process, requiring less mentalizing ability. However, these results were again only found in study 1. Including both groups in this contrast again generated no such results, which might point to a differential understanding of social inclusion/exclusion in autistic subjects. Nevertheless, this hypothesis is only preliminary and should be investigated in more detail in the future.

Regarding the effect of the EEB over both conditions and valences, i.e. the difference between congruent and incongruent trials, bilateral precuneus (study 1) as well as left dlPFC, bilateral precuneus and left angular gyrus (study 2) were enhanced, when the self and other experienced incongruent feeling states compared to congruent ones. In line with previous studies (Jackson, Brunet, Meltzoff, & Decety, 2006; Lamm et al., 2011; Silani et al., 2013), these regions correspond to cognitively adopting the perspective of another person by means of abstract visual information and distinguishing between oneself and other people. During incongruent emotional states, this switch of perspective is needed more strongly to correctly tag self- and other-related feelings. Interestingly, although these regions have mainly been indicated in the reflection of non-affective mental states of other people (Lamm & Majdandžić, 2015; Shamay-Tsoory, 2011), in the present study they were also activated when contemplating the *affective* state of another person, i.e. positive or negative. However, we did not find the right SMG, a region that had been suggested by a prior study to be activated during the overcoming of affective egocentric judgements using a similarly built paradigm to induce pleasant and unpleasant touch (Silani et al., 2013). Their findings can therefore not be generalized to feelings of social inclusion/exclusion within our sample.

Focusing on the specific hypotheses about the EEB differences depending on the emotional involvement of the self, the behavioral results could not be replicated on a neural level. Interestingly, the left SMG was activated to a stronger extent in the active condition compared to the passive condition when making congruent (in comparison to incongruent) judgements. This is surprising because of the involvement of its right-hemispheric counterpart in egocentricity and dealing with incongruence shown in the previous study by Silani et al. (2013). It could very well be that this region plays a more general role regarding the understanding of one's own in contrast to other's emotional states – may they be congruent or incongruent. One study also suggested bilateral involvement of SMG in multisensory integration during experimentally induced out-of-body experiences, a mechanism that is also concerned with the detection of mismatched external and internal signals (Ionta et al., 2011). Furthermore, Hoffmann et al. (2016) found marked patterns of connectivity of the right SMG to its left-hemispheric counterpart in a resting state-analysis. Findings on the role of the left SMG in processes of self-other-differentiation up to this point therefore remain rather mixed and unclear, and should constitute a focus of future investigations.

Another possible explanation, why regions related to overcoming egocentric judgements determined by Silani et al. (2013) were not found in the incongruent active condition, might be the amount of processing content of the conditions: During DOa, participants had to actively play as well as pay attention to their own feelings and those of another person, while they only had to pay attention to another player during DOp. A valid assumption might therefore be that the congruent trials were equally as demanding as the incongruent trials and this could have led to a lack of observed differences regarding hemodynamic activity in the active condition. Even though our prior hypothesis was that incongruent trials were associated with a greater difficulty in distinguishing self- and other-related feeling states, because the egocentric default has to be overcome and separated from the perspective of the other person (Bird & Viding, 2014; Decety, 2007), the same workload could have been necessary for congruent trials as well. Contrary to the findings of Silani et al. (2013), the found regions could play a role in the general appreciation of complex and demanding simultaneously experienced self- and other-related emotions, may they be congruent or incongruent. However, the behavioral data clearly showed increased egocentric judgements only during incongruent feelings of the self and another person. Future studies should therefore focus on carving out the similarities and differences of similar and dissimilar emotional states and the differential role of associated brain areas, especially for the right and left SMG.

Regions associated with executive functioning and working memory (caudate nucleus = CN; middle frontal gyrus = MFG), emotion regulation and valence evaluation (superior frontal gyrus = SFG; Lamm, Nusbaum, Meltzoff, & Decety, 2007) as well as affective empathy (inferior part of the orbitofrontal cortex (OFC); Decety, 2015; Reniers et al., 2014) also showed enhanced activation during incongruent trials. This is in line with the previously mentioned greater "effort" needed to overcome the own egocentric perspective as well as correctly identify, separate and then tag the distinct feelings of self and other. However, the majority of these results were found in study 2 with both control and ASD participants in one sample and the contrasts with only controls revealed nearly no enhanced activation. This might be due to the fact that neurotypicals indeed need less effort to overcome their own perspective in contrast to autistic participants, as shown on a descriptive level by the mean averages of the EEBs. In a second step, the occurrence of neurophysiological activation connected to egocentric judgements was therefore separately contrasted for the autistic participants to investigate if the found effects were mainly driven by the ASD group. The contrast *ASD incongruent > ASD congruent* revealed enhanced activation in dlPFC, SFG, inferior OFC, hippocampus and angular gyrus during incongruent trials. This might indeed indicate that autistic individuals recruit areas i.a. associated with mentalizing, emotion recognition/evaluation as well as affective empathy more strongly than controls when confronted with contrasting affective states of the self and other.

Regarding the hypotheses about group differences in study 2, we were also not able to replicate our behavioral effects and the findings of a previous study (Silani et al., 2013; see also Lamm et al., 2016). Autistic subjects did not show differential activation of areas related to overcoming the EEB in comparison to controls. Contrary to what we and others (Frith & De Vignemont, 2005) hypothesized, intact SOD and typically functioning rSMG connectivity in individuals with ASD was also reported by Hoffmann et al. (2016). On the other hand, impaired SOD has been linked to increased personal distress in individuals with ASD (Smith, 2008), which was also found by others (Sebastian et al., 2009) and in our sample: Autistic subjects reported significantly higher general personal distress than controls in an empathy questionnaire. In conclusion, other reasons could have prevented us from detecting differences in SOD between neurotypical and autistic individuals (see also next section). However, we did not assess self-reported or physiological symptoms of personal distress during the Cyberball game in our study. Future research should therefore focus on integrating measures of distress and other negative physiological effects into the investigation of emotional egocentricity in autism, for example via skin conductance, respiration, heart rate or other measures of arousal.

The present study has some limitations that could have contributed to the found results and should therefore be noted and discussed. For one, the first study investigated egocentric judgements only in male, right-handed participants to generate a homogeneous sample without handedness or gender as possible confounders. Especially the latter has been shown to exhibit clear differences in empathy, SOD and egocentricity on the behavioral as well as neural level (Christov-Moore et al., 2014). For example, Schulte-Rüther, Markowitsch, Shah, Fink, and Piefke (2008) found increased recruitment of mirror neurons during both self- and other-related processes in females and more left TPJ activity in males, suggesting that men and women rely on different strategies when processing emotions. Moreover, Tomova, Von Dawans, Heinrichs, Silani, and Lamm (2014) reported increased egocentricity in males under stress. As mentioned above, especially the factor of personal distress is crucial to keep in mind when investigating autism. The ASD sample in the second study also consisted mainly of male participants, because the disorder affects men to a greater extent (Lai et al., 2014). This means that the presented results can not readily be transferred to the general autistic population. A second limitation related to the participants was that the sample sizes of the two studies were relatively small. This might be one of the reasons why the group comparison did not show any differences on a behavioral as well as neural level. It would therefore be desirable to replicate the study in a larger sample and include a greater number of female participants to investigate similarities and differences regarding gender. Finally, the presented sample of ASD participants comprised only individuals with Asperger syndrome. It would be desirable to pursue the aims of this research in different subtypes of autism, e.g. also include individuals with high-functioning childhood autism and investigate differential effects. However, the recently published DSM-5 has newly defined Autism as a single diagnosis without subtypes (i.e. Autism-Spectrum-Disorder 299.0/F84.0; American Psychiatric Association, 2013), making any future research regarding different types of autistic individuals even more complex and challenging.

Secondly, although functional imaging techniques are one of the most used tools in social cognitive neuroscience, they are difficult to apply in situations that want to establish the feeling of interaction with at least one other person (Emery & Easton, 2005). Especially this interactive component that is essential to social cognition abilities (and therefore, tasks assessing social processes) is missing during an MRI scan. Even while watching videos of social interactions and reacting to them, the individual itself is not directly confronted with other people. A solution to this problem might therefore be live videos or games, connecting (or pretending to connect) the subject in the scanner with other people watching or playing simultaneously with the participant. Future studies should therefore focus on creating even more realistic, believable paradigms that constantly induce the actual presence of other people, for example using “live” videos of the players presented continuously on the screen or virtual reality.

In this context, the topic of believability should be mentioned. Apart from some exceptions, everybody guessed that they had actually played against a preset computer program when asked after their session. Zadro et al. (2004) investigated the necessary and sufficient conditions for experiencing feelings of exclusion during Cyberball and reported that participants felt bad even if they knew they were being excluded by a computer and not by other people. However, the adapted version implemented in the present study used a very strict game design due to the measurement of the EEB (i.e. alternating congruent and incongruent emotional states of inclusion and exclusion). This could have led to a high degree of predictability regarding the throws in the game and, in turn, to emotional detachment or even task disengagement from the social situation in the game (Bolling et al., 2011). In fact, many of the participants later reported feelings of monotony, boredom and some also indicated not feeling negatively affected by the manipulation, independent of them being in the control or ASD group. Moreover, many participants stated that they had tried to put themselves in the situation of a person experiencing such a game, but could only generate little to no emotional engagement. This is underlined by the fact that negative feelings of exclusion could only be shown on a behavioral level, but not fully mirrored in the neurophysiological data. Merely the control participants in study 1 showed some enhanced activation during exclusion of the other person; in study 2, the effects disappeared. Summarizing the reaction of the participants, an option for new studies using this adapted version of the Cyberball paradigm would be to introduce a greater amount of randomness and variability into the game, for example the usage of different time periods in waiting for the throws of the other people and varying times of all people "rating" each other. However, this version of Cyberball was conducted in a way to keep distractions to a minimum and increase fluent gameplay for autistic subjects. Future studies should therefore carefully weigh the importance of believability versus fluency against each other when designing the task.

Regarding the absence of effects in the neurophysiological data, one noticeable limitation might also have been the way, the functional data was preprocessed and analyzed. Firstly, we excluded the participants whose movements exceeded the set threshold, but some autistic subjects or matches of ASD participants were kept in the sample even though their movement patterns could have had an influence on the results. Secondly, a block design modeling the whole time of each video was chosen. However, this might have concealed underlying differences in hemodynamic activation that correspond only to certain situations during the video, e.g. the opposite person not getting the ball. Furthermore, the playing sequences could again have been too long, letting the negative effects/saliency of social exclusion and, in turn, its blood-oxygen-level-dependent

(BOLD) signal decrease over time. Therefore, one goal for subsequent analysis approaches will be to use different, more refined analysis methods like event-related designs and modeling only certain, relevant parts of the game in the model.

Finally, although our results clearly show strong negative judgements following exclusion and positive ones following inclusion, the gap between the behavioral and the neurophysiological results is wide and the reason for that is, up to this point, unclear. One other possibility is the factor of social desirability. Participants could have judged the other participants in a way that was expected of them (i.e. rating the other as negative because he did not get the ball). In fact, many participants reported that they were trying to put themselves in the social situation, but failed to feel emotionally affected by the events of the ball-game. Although such influences were strongly tried to be avoided, this should be considered as a limitation of the study. On the other hand, this would have lead the participants to always judge the other as negative, independent of what they themselves were experiencing. However, as indicated by our results, the participants showed considerable egocentricity on a behavioral level, which suggests some form of real first-hand emotional involvement in the task and attempts to overcome egocentricity.

In conclusion, the present study promotes robust behavioral evidence for the occurrence of empathic judgements biased by egocentricity in both healthy and autistic adults. However, no differences between the two groups could be observed in this sample, indicating similar ability for SOD to overcome egocentric shifts in the direction of one's own emotional state. Taken together, this thesis has begun to add valuable insights to the research of social processes related to self-other distinction and emotional egocentricity in neurotypical as well as the autistic population. However, clear distinctions between different concepts of empathy and mentalizing are needed to clarify impairments in ASD. Investigating such crucial concepts on a more basic level with valid paradigms will ultimately pave the way to better understand autistic individuals and could set the foundation for interventions targeting positive and successful interactions with other people – may these be with autistic or non-autistic individuals.

References

Abrams, D., Hogg, M. A., & Marques, J. M. (2005). A social psychological framework for understanding social inclusion and exclusion. In D. Abrams, M. A. Hogg, & J. M. Marques (Eds.), *The Social Psycholody of Inclusion and Exclusion* (pp. 1–23). New York, NY: Psychology Press.

Abrams, D., Weick, M., Thomas, D., Colbe, H., & Franklin, K. M. (2011). On-line ostracism affects children differently from adolescents and adults. *The British Journal of Developmental Psychology*, *29*, 110–123. http://doi.org/10.1348/026151010X494089

American Psychiatric Association. (2000). *Diagnostic and Statistical Manual of Mental Disorders (DSM-IV-TR)* (4th ed.). Washington, DC: American Psychiatric Publishing.

American Psychiatric Association. (2013). *Diagnostic and Statistical Manual of Mental Disorders (DSM-5)* (5th ed.). Washington, DC: American Psychiatric Publishing.

Baars, B. J., & Gage, N. M. (2010). *Cognition, brain and consciousness. Introduction to cognitive neuroscience* (2nd ed.). Burlington, MA: Academic Press.

Bach, M., Bach, D., de Zwaan, M., & Serim, M. (1996). Validierung der deutschen Version der 20-Item Toronto-Alexithymie-Skala bei Normalpersonen und psychiatrischen Patienten. *PPmP: Psychotherapie*, 208–214.

Bagby, R. M., Parker, J. D. A., & Taylor, G. J. (1994). The twenty-item Toronto Alexithymia scale-I. Item selection and cross-validation of the factor structure. *Journal of Psychosomatic Research*, *38*(1), 23–32. http://doi.org/10.1016/0022-3999(94)90005-1

Baron-Cohen, S. (2005). Autism and the origins of social neuroscience. In A. Easton & N. J. Emery (Eds.), *The Cognitive Neuroscience of Social Behaviour* (pp. 240–255). Hove, East Sussex: Psychology Press.

Baron-Cohen, S., Wheelwright, S. J., Skinner, R., Martin, J., & Clubley, E. (2001). The Autism Spectrum Quotient: Evidence from Asperger syndrome/high functioning autism, males and females, scientists and mathematicians. *Journal of Autism and Developmental Disorders*, *31*, 5–17. http://doi.org/10.1023/A:1005653411471

Batson, C. D. (2009). These things called empathy: Eight related but distinct phenomena. In J. Decety & W. Ickes (Eds.), *The Social Neuroscience of Empathy* (pp. 3–16). Cambridge, MA: MIT Press.

Bernhardt, B. C., & Singer, T. (2012). The neural basis of empathy. *Annual Review of Neuroscience*, *35*(1), 1–23. http://doi.org/10.1146/annurev-neuro-062111-150536

Bird, G., & Cook, R. (2013). Mixed emotions: the contribution of alexithymia to the emotional symptoms of autism. *Translational Psychiatry*, *3*(7). http://doi.org/10.1038/tp.2013.61

Bird, G., Silani, G., Brindley, R., White, S., Frith, U., & Singer, T. (2010). Empathic brain responses in insula are modulated by levels of alexithymia but not autism. *Brain*, *133*(5), 1515–1525. http://doi.org/10.1093/brain/awq060

H. Hartmann, *Social Interactions in Autism*, BestMasters,
https://doi.org/10.1007/978-3-658-22013-6

Bird, G., & Viding, E. (2014). The self to other model of empathy: Providing a new framework for understanding empathy impairments in psychopathy, autism, and alexithymia. *Neuroscience & Biobehavioral Reviews*, *47*, 520–532. http://doi.org/10.1016/j.neubiorev.2014.09.021

Blair, R. J. R., Frith, U., Smith, N., Abell, F., & Cipolotti, L. (2002). Fractionation of visual memory: Agency detection and its impairment in autism. *Neuropsychologia*, *40*(1), 108–118. http://doi.org/10.1016/S0028-3932(01)00069-0

Bolling, D. Z., Pitskel, N. B., Deen, B., Crowley, M. J., & McPartland, J. C. (2011). Enhanced neural responses to rule violation in children with autism: A comparison to social exclusion. *Developmental Cognitive Neuroscience*, *1*(3), 280–294. http://doi.org/10.1016/j.dcn.2011.02.002.Enhanced

Booth, J. R., Wood, L., Lu, D., Houk, J. C., & Bitan, T. (2007). The role of the basal ganglia and cerebellum in language processing. *Brain Research*, *1133*(1), 136–144. http://doi.org/10.1016/j.brainres.2006.11.074

Catmur, C., Cross, E. S., & Over, H. (2016). Understanding self and others: From origins to disorders. *Philosophical Transactions of the Royal Society of London. Series B, Biological Sciences*, *371*(1686), 20150066. http://doi.org/10.1098/rstb.2015.0066

Christov-Moore, L., Simpson, E. A., Coudé, G., Grigaityte, K., Iacoboni, M., & Ferrari, P. F. (2014). Empathy: Gender effects in brain and behavior, *46*, 604–627. http://doi.org/10.1016/j.neubiorev.2014.09.001.Empathy

Corradi-Dell'Acqua, C., Tusche, A., Vuilleumier, P., & Singer, T. (2016). Cross-modal representations of first-hand and vicarious pain, disgust and fairness in insular and cingulate cortex. *Nature Communications*, *7*, 10904. http://doi.org/10.1038/ncomms10904

Davis, M. H. (1980). A Multidimensional Approach to Individual Differences in Empathy. *JSAS Catalog of Selected Documents in Psychology*, *10*, 85.

de Guzman, M., Bird, G., Banissy, M. J., & Catmur, C. (2015). Self-other control processes in social cognition: From imitation to empathy. *Philosophical Transactions of the Royal Society B: Biological Sciences*, *371*, 20150079. http://dx.doi.org/ 10.1098/rstb.2015.0079

de Vignemont, F., & Singer, T. (2006). The empathic brain: How, when and why? *Trends in Cognitive Sciences*, *10*(10), 435–441. http://doi.org/10.1016/j.tics.2006.08.008

de Waal, F. B. M. (2008). Putting the altruism back into altruism: the evolution of empathy. *Annual Review of Psychology*, *59*, 279–300. http://doi.org/10.1146/annurev.psych.59.103006.093625

Decety, J. (2007). A social cognitive neuroscience model of human empathy. In E. Harmon-Jones & P. Winkielman (Eds.), *Social Neuroscience. Integrating Biological and Psychological Explanations of Social Behavior* (pp. 246–270). New York, NY: The Guilford Press.

Decety, J. (2015). The neural pathways, development and functions of empathy. *Current Opinion in Behavioral Sciences*, *3*, 1–6. http://doi.org/10.1016/j.cobeha.2014.12.001

Decety, J., & Chaminade, T. (2003). When the self represents the other: A new cognitive neuroscience view on psychological identification. *Consciousness and Cognition*, *12*(4), 577–596. http://doi.org/10.1016/S1053-8100(03)00076-X

Decety, J., & Grèzes, J. (2006). The power of simulation: Imagining one's own and other's behavior. *Brain Research, 1079*(1), 4–14. http://doi.org/10.1016/j.brainres.2005.12.115

Decety, J., & Lamm, C. (2009). Empathy versus personal distress: Recent evidence from social neuroscience. In J. Decety & W. Ickes (Eds.), *The Social Neuroscience of Empathy* (pp. 199–213). Cambridge, MA: MIT Press.

Decety, J., & Michalska, K. (2013). A neuroscience perspective on empathy and its development. *Neural Circuit Development and Function in the Brain: Comprehensive Developmental Neuroscience, 3*, 379–393. http://doi.org/10.1016/B978-0-12-397267-5.00026-1

Decety, J., & Sommerville, J. A. (2003). Shared representations between self and other: A social cognitive neuroscience view. *Trends in Cognitive Sciences, 7*(12), 527–533. http://doi.org/10.1016/j.tics.2003.10.004

Delaney, H. D., & Maxwell, S. E. (1981). On Using Analysis of Covariance in Repeated Measures Designs. *Multivariate Behavioral Research, 16*(1), 105–123. http://doi.org/10.1207/s15327906mbr1601_6

Dziobek, I., Rogers, K., Fleck, S., Bahnemann, M., Heekeren, H. R., Wolf, O. T., & Convit, A. (2008). Dissociation of cognitive and emotional empathy in adults with Asperger syndrome using the Multifaceted Empathy Test (MET). *Journal of Autism and Developmental Disorders, 38*(3), 464–473. http://doi.org/10.1007/s10803-007-0486-x

Eisenberger, N. I. (2011). Why rejection hurts: What social neuroscience has revealed about the brain's response to social rejection. In J. Decety & J. T. Cacioppo (Eds.), *The Handbook of Social Neuroscience* (pp. 109–127). New York, NY: Oxford University Press. http://doi.org/10.1093/oxfordhb/9780195342161.013.0039

Eisenberger, N. I. (2012). The pain of social disconnection: Examining the shared neural underpinnings of physical and social pain. *Nature Reviews: Neuroscience, 13*(6), 421–34. http://doi.org/10.1038/nrn3231

Eisenberger, N. I. (2015). Social pain and the brain: Controversies, questions, and where to go from here. *Annual Review of Psychology, 66*(1). http://doi.org/10.1146/annurev-psych-010213-115146

Eisenberger, N. I., Lieberman, M. D., & Williams, K. D. (2003). Does rejection hurt? An fMRI study of social exclusion. *Science, 302*(290), 290–292. http://doi.org/10.1126/science.1089134

Emery, N. J. (2005). The evolution of social cognition. In A. Easton & N. J. Emery (Eds.), *The Cognitive Neuroscience of Social Behaviour* (pp. 115–156). Hove, East Sussex: Psychology Press.

Emery, N. J., & Easton, A. (2005). Introduction: What is social cognitive neuroscience (SCN)? In A. Easton & N. J. Emery (Eds.), *The Cognitive Neuroscience of Social Behaviour* (pp. 1–16). Hove, East Sussex: Psychology Press.

Epley, N., Keysar, B., van Boven, L., & Gilovich, T. (2004). Perspective taking as egocentric anchoring and adjustment. *Journal of Personality and Social Psychology, 87*(3), 327–339. http://doi.org/10.1037/0022-3514.87.3.327

Epley, N., Morewedge, C. K., & Keysar, B. (2004). Perspective taking in children and adults: Equivalent egocentrism but differential correction. *Journal of Experimental Social Psychology*, *40*(6), 760–768. http://doi.org/10.1016/j.jesp.2004.02.002

Fan, Y. T., Chen, C., Chen, S. C., Decety, J., & Cheng, Y. (2014). Empathic arousal and social understanding in individuals with autism: Evidence from fMRI and ERP measurements. *Social Cognitive and Affective Neuroscience*, *9*(8). http://doi.org/10.1093/scan/nst101

Freitag, C. M., Retz-Junginger, P., Retz, W., Seitz, C., Palmason, H., Meyer, J., ... von Gontard, A. (2015). Evaluation der deutschen Version des Autismus-Spektrum-Quotienten (AQ) - die Kurzversion AQ-K. *Zeitschrift Für Klinische Psychologie Und Psychotherapie*, *36*, 280–289. http://doi.org/10.1026/1616-3443.36.4.280

Frith, C. D. (2008). Social cognition. *Philosophical Transactions of the Royal Society B: Biological Sciences*, *363*(1499), 2033–2039. http://doi.org/10.1098/rstb.2008.0005

Frith, U., & de Vignemont, F. (2005). Egocentrism, allocentrism, and Asperger syndrome. *Consciousness and Cognition*, *14*(4), 719–738. http://doi.org/10.1016/j.concog.2005.04.006

Goldings, H. J. (1954). On the avowal and projection of happiness. *Journal of Personality*, *23*, 30–47.

Goubert, L., Craig, K. D., & Buysse, A. (2009). Perceiving others in pain: Experimental and clinical evidence on the role of empathy. In J. Decety & W. Ickes (Eds.), *The Social Neuroscience of Empathy* (pp. 153–165). Cambridge, MA: MIT Press.

Grossman, E. D., & Blake, R. (2002). Brain areas active during visual perception of biological motion. *Neuron*, *35*(6), 1167–1175. http://doi.org/10.1016/S0896-6273(02)00897-8

Gu, X., Eilam-Stock, T., Zhou, T., Anagnostou, E., Kolevzon, A., Soorya, L., ... Fan, J. (2015). Autonomic and brain responses associated with empathy deficits in autism spectrum disorder. *Human Brain Mapping*, *36*, 3323–3338. http://doi.org/10.1002/hbm.22840

Harmon-Jones, E., & Beer, J. S. (2009). Introduction to social and personality neuroscience methods. In E. Harmon-Jones & J. S. Beer (Eds.), *Methods in Social Neuroscience* (pp. 1–9). New York, NY: The Guilford Press.

Hartgerink, C. H. J., van Beest, I., Wicherts, J. M., & Williams, K. D. (2015). The ordinal effects of ostracism: a meta-analysis of 120 Cyberball studies. *PloS One*, *10*(5), e0127002. http://doi.org/10.1371/journal.pone.0127002

Heberlein, A. S., & Adolphs, R. (2005). Functional anatomy of human social cognition. In A. Easton & N. J. Emery (Eds.), *The Cognitive Neuroscience of Social Behaviour* (pp. 157–194). Hove, East Sussex: Psychology Press.

Hitz, H. (2017). *Empathic competences during social interactions in Autism Spectrum Disorder – an fMRI study*. Unpublished master thesis. Faculty of Psychology. University of Vienna.

Hoffmann, F., Koehne, S., Steinbeis, N., Dziobek, I., & Singer, T. (2016). Preserved self-other distinction during empathy in autism is linked to network integrity of right supramarginal gyrus. *Journal of Autism and Developmental Disorders*, *46*(2), 637–648. http://doi.org/10.1007/s10803-015-2609-0

Ickes, W. (2009). Empathic accuracy: Its links to clinical, cognitive, developmental, social, and physiological psychology. In J. Decety & W. Ickes (Eds.), *The Social Neuroscience of Empathy* (pp. 57–70). Cambridge, MA: MIT Press.

Ionta, S., Heydrich, L., Lenggenhager, B., Mouthon, M., Fornari, E., Chapuis, D., ... Blanke, O. (2011). Multisensory Mechanisms in Temporo-Parietal Cortex Support Self-Location and First-Person Perspective. *Neuron*, *70*(2), 363–374. http://doi.org/10.1016/j.neuron.2011.03.009

Jackson, P. L., Brunet, E., Meltzoff, A. N., & Decety, J. (2006). Empathy examined through the neural mechanisms involved in imagining how I feel versus how you feel pain. *Neuropsychologia*, *44*(5), 752–761. http://doi.org/10.1016/j.neuropsychologia.2005.07.015

Jackson, P. L., Rainville, P., & Decety, J. (2006, November). To what extent do we share the pain of others? Insight from the neural bases of pain empathy. *Pain*. http://doi.org/10.1016/j.pain.2006.09.013

Johnstone, T., Kim, J. M., & Whalen, P. J. (2009). Functional magnetic resonance imaging in the affective and social neurosciences. In E. Harmon-Jones & J. S. Beer (Eds.), *Methods in Social Neuroscience* (pp. 313–336). New York, NY: The Guilford Press.

Klin, A., Jones, W., Schultz, R., Volkmar, F., & Cohen, D. (2002). Visual fixation patterns during viewing of naturalistic social situations as predictors of social competence in individuals with autism. *Archives of General Psychiatry*, *59*(9), 809–816. http://doi.org/10.1001/archpsyc.59.9.809

Krach, S., Kamp-Becker, I., Einhäuser, W., Sommer, J., Frässle, S., Jansen, A., ... Paulus, F. M. (2015). Evidence from pupillometry and fMRI indicates reduced neural response during vicarious social pain but not physical pain in autism. *Human Brain Mapping*, *36*(11), 4730–4744. http://doi.org/10.1002/hbm.22949

Krämer, U. M., Mohammadi, B., Doñamayor, N., Samii, A., & Münte, T. F. (2010). Emotional and cognitive aspects of empathy and their relation to social cognition - an fMRI-study. *Brain Research*, *1311*, 110–120. http://doi.org/10.1016/j.brainres.2009.11.043

Kratzmeier, H., & Horn, R. (1988). Standard Progressive Matrices (SPM). Test Manual. Beltz Test.

Kühner, P. D. C., Bürger, C., Keller, F., & Hautzinger, M. (2007). Reliabilität und Validität des revidierten Beck-Depressionsinventars (BDI-II). *Der Nervenarzt*, *78*(6), 651–656.

Lai, M.-C., Lombardo, M. V., & Baron-Cohen, S. (2014). Autism. *The Lancet*, *383*(9920), 896–910. http://doi.org/10.1016/S0140-6736(13)61539-1

Lamm, C., Bukowski, H., & Silani, G. (2016). From shared to distinct self-other representations in empathy: Evidence from neurotypical function and socio-cognitive disorders. *Philosophical Transactions of the Royal Society of London. Series B, Biological Sciences*, *371*(1686). http://doi.org/10.1098/rstb.2015.0083

Lamm, C., Decety, J., & Singer, T. (2011). Meta-analytic evidence for common and distinct neural networks associated with directly experienced pain and empathy for pain. *NeuroImage*, *54*(3), 2492–2502. http://doi.org/10.1016/j.neuroimage.2010.10.014

Lamm, C., & Majdandžić, J. (2015). The role of shared neural activations, mirror neurons, and morality in empathy - A critical comment. *Neuroscience Research*, *90*, 15–24. http://doi.org/10.1016/j.neures.2014.10.008

Lamm, C., Nusbaum, H. C., Meltzoff, A. N., & Decety, J. (2007). What are you feeling? Using functional magnetic resonance imaging to assess the modulation of sensory and affective responses during empathy for pain. *PLoS ONE*, *2*(12). http://doi.org/10.1371/journal.pone.0001292

Lehrl, S. (1995). Mehrfachwahl-Wortschatz-Intelligenztest (MWT-B). Balingen: PERIMED-spitta.

Lewis, M., & Brooks-Gunn, J. (1979). *Social cognition and the acquisition of self*. New York, NY: Plenum Press.

Lieberman, M. D., & Pfeifer, J. H. (2005). The self and social perception: Three kinds of questions in social cognitive neuroscience. In A. Easton & N. J. Emery (Eds.), *The Cognitive Neuroscience of Social Behaviour* (pp. 195–235). Hove, East Sussex: Psychology Press.

Lockwood, P. L. (2016). The anatomy of empathy: Vicarious experience and disorders of social cognition. *Behavioural Brain Research*. http://doi.org/10.1016/j.bbr.2016.05.048

Lockwood, P. L., Bird, G., Bridge, M., & Viding, E. (2013). Dissecting empathy: high levels of psychopathic and autistic traits are characterized by difficulties in different social information processing domains. *Frontiers in Human Neuroscience*, *7*. http://doi.org/10.3389/fnhum.2013.00760

Lombardo, M. V., Barnes, J. L., Wheelwright, S. J., & Baron-Cohen, S. (2007). Self-referential cognition and empathy in autism. *PLOS ONE*, *2*(9), e883. http://doi.org/10.1371/journal.pone.0000883

Lombardo, M. V., Chakrabarti, B., Bullmore, E. T., Sadek, S. A., Pasco, G., Wheelwright, S. J., ... Baron-Cohen, S. (2009). Atypical neural self-representation in autism. *Brain*, *133*(2), 611–624. http://doi.org/10.1093/brain/awp306

Luyten, P., & Fonagy, P. (2015). The neurobiology of mentalizing. *Psychotherapy*, *6*(4), 366–379. http://doi.org/10.1037/per0000117

Maddock, R. J. (1999). The retrosplenial cortex and emotion: new insights from functional neuroimaging of the human brain. *Trends in Neurosciences*, *22*(7), 310–316. http://doi.org/10.1016/S0166-2236(98)01374-5

Martínez, A., Anllo-Vento, L., Sereno, M. I., Frank, L. R., Buxton, R. B., Dubowitz, D. J., ... Hillyard, S. A. (1999). Involvement of striate and extrastriate visual cortical areas in spatial attention. *Nature Neuroscience*, *2*(4), 364–369. http://doi.org/10.1038/7274

Masten, C. L., & Colich, N. L. (2011). An fMRI investigation of responses to peer rejection in adolescents with autism spectrum disorders. *Developmental Cognitive Neuroscience*, *1*(3), 260–270. http://doi.org/10.1016/j.dcn.2011.01.004.An

Mazza, M., Pino, M. C., Mariano, M., Tempesta, D., Ferrara, M., de Berardis, D., ... Valenti, M. (2014). Affective and cognitive empathy in adolescents with autism spectrum disorder. *Frontiers in Human Neuroscience*, *8*, 791. http://doi.org/10.3389/fnhum.2014.00791

Nickerson, R. S., Butler, S. F., & Carlin, M. (2009). Empathy and knowledge projection. In J. Decety & W. Ickes (Eds.), *The Social Neuroscience of Empathy* (pp. 43–56). Cambridge, MA: MIT Press.

Norris, C. J., & Cacioppo, J. T. (2007). I know how you feel. Social and emotional information processing in the brain. In E. Harmon-Jones & P. Winkielman (Eds.), *Social Neuroscience. Integrating Biological and Psychological Explanations of Social Behavior* (pp. 84–105). New York, NY: The Guilford Press.

Novembre, G., Zanon, M., & Silani, G. (2015). Empathy for social exclusion involves the sensory-discriminative component of pain: A within-subject fMRI study. *Social, Cognitive and Affective Neuroscience, 10*(2), 153–164. http://doi.org/10.1093/scan/nsu038

Oberhuber, M., Jones, 'Ōiwi Parker, Hope, T. M. H., Prejawa, S., Seghier, M. L., Green, D. W., & Price, C. J. (2013). Functionally distinct contributions of the anterior and posterior putamen during sublexical and lexical reading. *Frontiers in Human Neuroscience, 7*(November), 787. http://doi.org/10.3389/fnhum.2013.00787

Ochsner, K. N., Zaki, J., Hanelin, J., Ludlow, D. H., Knierim, K., Ramachandran, T., ... Mackey, S. C. (2008). Your pain or mine? Common and distinct neural systems supporting the perception of pain in self and other. *Social, Cognitive and Affective Neuroscience, 3*(2), 144–160. http://doi.org/10.1093/scan/nsn006

Preston, S. D., & de Waal, F. B. M. (2002). Empathy: Its ultimate and proximate bases. *Behavioral & Brain Sciences, 25*, 1–72.

Pronin, E. (2008). How we see ourselves and how we see others. *Science, 320*, 1177–1181.

Rajah, M. N., Languay, R., & Grady, C. L. (2011). Age-related changes in right middle frontal gyrus volume correlate with altered episodic retrieval acctivity. *Journal of Neuroscience, 31*(49), 17941–17954. http://doi.org/10.1523/JNEUROSCI.1690-11.2011

Reniers, R. L. E. P., Völlm, B. A., Elliott, R., & Corcoran, R. (2014). Empathy, ToM, and self-other differentiation: An fMRI study of internal states. *Social Neuroscience, 9*(1), 50–62. http://doi.org/10.1080/17470919.2013.861360

Riva, F., Triscoli, C., Lamm, C., Carnaghi, A., & Silani, G. (2016). Emotional egocentricity bias across the life-span. *Frontiers in Aging Neuroscience, 8*, 1–7. http://doi.org/10.3389/fnagi.2016.00074

Rogers, K., Dziobek, I., Hassenstab, J., Wolf, O. T., & Convit, A. (2007). Who cares? Revisiting empathy in Asperger syndrome. *Journal of Autism and Developmental Disorders, 37*(4), 709–715. http://doi.org/10.1007/s10803-006-0197-8

Royzman, E. B., Cassidy, K. W., & Baron, J. (2003). "I know, you know": Epistemic egocentrism in children and adults. *Review of General Psychology, 7*(1), 38–65. http://doi.org/10.1037/1089-2680.7.1.38

Rütgen, M., Seidel, E.-M., Silani, G., Riecansky, I., Hummer, A., Windischberger, C., ... Lamm, C. (2015). Placebo analgesia and its opioidergic regulation suggest that empathy for pain is grounded in self pain. *PNAS*, E5638–E5646. http://doi.org/10.1073/pnas.1511269112

Schulte-Ruether, M., Greimel, E., Piefke, M., Kamp-Becker, I., Remschmidt, H., Fink, G. R., ... Konrad, K. (2014). Age-dependent changes in the neural substrates of empathy in autism spectrum disorder. *Social, Cognitive and Affective Neuroscience, 9*(8), 1118–1126. http://doi.org/10.1093/scan/nst088

Schulte-Ruether, M., Markowitsch, H. J., Shah, N. J., Fink, G. R., & Piefke, M. (2008). Gender differences in brain networks supporting empathy. *NeuroImage*, *42*(1), 393–403. http://doi.org/10.1016/j.neuroimage.2008.04.180

Sebastian, C. L., Blakemore, S.-J., & Charman, T. (2009). Reactions to ostracism in adolescents with autism spectrum conditions. *Journal of Autism and Developmental Disorders*, *39*(8), 1122–1130. http://doi.org/10.1007/s10803-009-0725-4

Sebastian, C. L., Fontaine, N. M. G., Bird, G., Blakemore, S.-J., de Brito, S. A., McCrory, E. J. P., & Viding, E. (2012). Neural processing associated with cognitive and affective Theory of Mind in adolescents and adults. *Social, Cognitive and Affective Neuroscience*, *7*(1), 53–63. http://doi.org/10.1093/scan/nsr023

Servos, P., Osu, R., Santi, A., & Kawato, M. (2002). The neural substrates of biological motion perception: an fMRI study. *Cerebral Cortex (New York, N.Y. : 1991)*, *12*(7), 772–782. http://doi.org/10.1093/cercor/12.7.772

Shamay-Tsoory, S. G. (2009). Empathic processing: Its cognitive and affective dimensions and neuroanatomical basis. In J. Decety & W. Ickes (Eds.), *The Social Neuroscience of Empathy* (pp. 215–232). Cambridge, MA: MIT Press.

Shamay-Tsoory, S. G. (2011). The neural bases for empathy. *The Neuroscientist*, *17*(1), 18–24. http://doi.org/10.1177/1073858410379268

Shamay-Tsoory, S. G. (2014). Dynamic functional integration of distinct neural empathy systems. *Social, Cognitive and Affective Neuroscience*, *9*(1), 1–2. http://doi.org/10.1093/scan/nst107

Silani, G., Bird, G., Brindley, R., Singer, T., Frith, C. D., & Frith, U. (2008). Levels of emotional awareness and autism: An fMRI study. *Social Neuroscience*, *3*(2), 97–112. http://doi.org/10.1080/17470910701577020

Silani, G., Lamm, C., Ruff, C. C., & Singer, T. (2013). Right supramarginal gyrus is crucial to overcome emotional egocentricity bias in social judgments. *Journal of Neuroscience*, *33*(39), 15466–15476. http://doi.org/10.1523/JNEUROSCI.1488-13.2013

Singer, T. (2006). The neuronal basis and ontogeny of empathy and mind reading: Review of literature and implications for future research. *Neuroscience & Biobehavioral Reviews*, *30*(6), 855–863. http://doi.org/10.1016/j.neubiorev.2006.06.011

Singer, T., & Lamm, C. (2009). The social neuroscience of empathy. *Annals of the New York Academy of Sciences*, *1156*(1), 81–96. http://doi.org/10.1111/j.1749-6632.2009.04418.x

Singer, T., Seymour, B., O'Doherty, J., Dolan, R. J., Kaube, H., & Frith, C. D. (2004). Empathy for pain involves the affective but not sensory components of pain. *Science*, *303*(5661), 1157–1162. http://doi.org/10.1126/science.1093535

Smith, A. (2008). The empathy imbalance hypothesis of autism: A theoretical approach to cognitive and emotional empathy in autistic development. *Psychological Record*, *59*(2), 489–509.

Steinbeis, N. (2016). The role of self–other distinction in understanding others' mental and emotional states: Neurocognitive mechanisms in children and adults. *Philosophical Transactions of the Royal Society B: Biological Sciences*, *371*, 20150074. http://doi.org/10.1098/rstb.2015.0074

Steinbeis, N., Bernhardt, B. C., & Singer, T. (2015). Age-related differences in function and structure of rSMG and reduced functional connectivity with DLPFC explains heightened emotional egocentricity bias in childhood. *Social, Cognitive and Affective Neuroscience, 10*, 302–310. http://doi.org/10.1093/scan/nsu057

Steinbeis, N., & Singer, T. (2014). Projecting my envy onto you: Neurocognitive mechanisms of an offline emotional egocentricity bias. *NeuroImage*. http://doi.org/10.1016/j.neuroimage.2014.08.007

Stepnicka, P. H. (2016). *Simulating social pain - behavioral evidences of Emotional Egocentricity Bias and Self-Other Distinction in empathic processing*. Unpublished master thesis, University of Vienna. Faculty of Psychology.

Surtees, A. D. R., & Apperly, I. A. (2012). Egocentrism and automatic perspective taking in children and adults. *Child Development, 83*(2), 452–460. http://doi.org/10.1111/j.1467-8624.2011.01730.x

Taubner, S. (2015). *Konzept Mentalisieren - Eine Einführung in Forschung und Praxis*. Gießen: Psychosozial-Verlag.

Thirioux, B., Mercier, M. R., Blanke, O., & Berthoz, A. (2014). The cognitive and neural time course of empathy and sympathy: An electrical neuroimaging study on self-other interaction. *Neuroscience, 267*, 286–306. http://doi.org/10.1016/j.neuroscience.2014.02.024

Tomova, L., Von Dawans, B., Heinrichs, M., Silani, G., & Lamm, C. (2014). Is stress affecting our ability to tune into others? Evidence for gender differences in the effects of stress on self-other distinction. *Psychoneuroendocrinology, 43*, 95–104. http://doi.org/10.1016/j.psyneuen.2014.02.006

Tracey, I., & Mantyh, P. W. (2007). The Cerebral Signature for Pain Perception and Its Modulation. *Neuron, 55*(3), 377–391. http://doi.org/10.1016/j.neuron.2007.07.012

van Baaren, R. B., Decety, J., Dijksterhuis, A., van der Leij, A., & van Leeuwen, M. L. (2009). Being imitated: Consequences of nonconciously showing empathy. In J. Decety & W. Ickes (Eds.), *The Social Neuroscience of Empathy* (pp. 31–42). Cambridge, MA: MIT Press.

van Veluw, S. J., & Chance, S. A. (2014). Differentiating between self and others: An ALE meta-analysis of fMRI studies of self-recognition and theory of mind. *Brain Imaging and Behavior, 8*(1), 24–38. http://doi.org/10.1007/s11682-013-9266-8

Walter, H. (2012). Social cognitive neuroscience of empathy – concepts, circuits and genes. *Neuroscience, 4*(1), 9–17. http://doi.org/10.1177/1754073911421379

Williams, K. D. (2007). Ostracism. *Annual Review of Psychology, 58*(1), 425–452. http://doi.org/10.1146/annurev.psych.58.110405.085641

Williams, K. D., Cheung, C. K., & Choi, W. (2000). Cyberostracism: Effects of being ignored over the internet. *Journal of Personality and Social Psychology, 79*(5), 748–762. http://doi.org/10.1037/0022-3514.79.5.748

Williams, K. D., & Jarvis, B. (2006). Cyberball: A program for use in research on interpersonal ostracism and acceptance. *Behavior Research Methods, 38*(1), 174–180. http://doi.org/10.3758/BF03192765

Woo, C.-W., Koban, L., Kross, E., Lindquist, M. A., Banich, M. T., Ruzic, L., ... Wager, T. D. (2014). Separate neural representations for physical pain and social rejection. *Nature Communications*, *5*, 5380. http://doi.org/10.1038/ncomms6380

Woo, C.-W., Krishnan, A., & Wager, T. D. (2014). Cluster-extent based thresholding in fMRI analyses: Pitfalls and recommendations. *NeuroImage*, *91*, 412–419. http://doi.org/10.1016/j.neuroimage.2013.12.058

Yousry, T. A., Schmid, U. D., Alkadhi, H., Schmidt, D., Peraud, A., Buettner, A., & Winkler, P. (1997). Localization of the motor hand area to a knob on the precentral gyrus. A new landmark. *Brain*, *120*(1), 141–157. http://doi.org/10.1093/brain/120.1.141

Zadro, L., Williams, K. D., & Richardson, R. (2004). How low can you go? Ostracism by a computer is sufficient to lower self-reported levels of belonging, control, self-esteem, and meaningful existence. *Journal of Experimental Social Psychology*, *40*(4), 560–567. http://doi.org/10.1016/j.jesp.2003.11.006

Zaki, J., & Ochsner, K. N. (2012). The neuroscience of empathy: Progress, pitfalls and promise. *Nature Neuroscience*, *15*(5), 675–680. http://doi.org/10.1038/nn.3085

Appendix

Appendix I

Additional tables for study 1 are presented.

Table A1
Descriptive Statistics for depression, trait empathy and alexithymia of the participants in study 1.

Questionnaires	*M (SD)*
Depression	6.85 (7.32)
Trait Empathy	
Fantasy	3.05 (0.64)
Empathic Concern	3.56 (0.63)
Perspective Taking	3.60 (0.48)
Personal Distress	2.49 (0.55)
Alexithymia	
Difficulty Identifying Feelings	12.75 (5.72)
Difficulty Describing Feelings	12.45 (3.86)
Externally Oriented Thinking	17.00 (4.38)

Note. Means and standard deviations are given.

Table A2
Spearman correlations between the mean EEBs, alexithymia, trait empathy and autistic traits in study 1.

	Active EEB	Passive EEB	Diff EEB	Autistic traits
Alexithymia				
Difficulty Identifying Feelings	-.28	**-.65***	.06	.34
Difficulty Describing Feelings	< .01	-.34	-.07	.12
Externally Oriented Thinking	.10	-.13	.04	**.45***
Overall Score	-.09	-.44	.01	.35
Trait empathy				
Fantasy	-.22	-.31	.03	-.20
Empathic Concern	-.22	-.08	-.16	-.33
Perspective Taking	-.06	.22	-.06	**-.56***
Personal Distress	.06	-.11	.24	.36
Autistic traits	.29	-.24	**.45***	----

Note. Correlations were calculated two-sided. The difference was calculated by subtracting the mean passive EEB from the mean active EEB. Significant correlations ($p < .05$) are marked with an asterisk. The sample size for study 1 was $n_1 = 20$.

H. Hartmann, *Social Interactions in Autism*, BestMasters,
https://doi.org/10.1007/978-3-658-22013-6

Table A3
Main effects and interactions of the repeated measures ANOVA (Pillai-Spur) of the average rating time in study 1.

Factors	$F_{(1,19)}$	p	η_p^2
condition	3.869	.064	0.169
valence	3.845	.064	0.169
congruency	10.572	.004	0.358
condition x valence	0.221	.644	0.011
condition x congruency	0.365	.553	0.019
valence x congruency	0.083	.776	0.004
condition x valence x congruency	0.030	.865	0.002

Note. The ANOVA was calculated with the within-subject factors condition (active vs. passive), valence (inclusion vs. exclusion) and congruency (congruent vs. incongruent). Level of significance: $p < .05$.

Table A4
Main effect of valence (Other inclusion > exclusion) in study 1.

Anatomical Region	H	cluster K	T	Z score	x, y, z
Middle temporal gyrus	R	123	3.65	3.56	56, -60, 8
Fusiform gyrus	R	19	3.52	3.44	28, -82, -6

Note. H = hemisphere. Uncorrected level of significance level $p = .001$. Coordinates are given in mm.

Table A5

Main effect of congruency (congruent > incongruent) in study 1.

Anatomical Region	H	cluster K	*T*	Z score	x, y, z
Putamen	L	101	4.00	3.88	-24, 0, 8
Putamen	L		3.72	3.62	-26, 16, 0
Putamen	L		3.39	3.31	-30, 0, -4
Putamen	R	74	3.67	3.58	24, 16, 0
Putamen	R		3.46	3.38	26, 10, 8
Lingual gyrus	L	195	3.94	3.83	-16, -54, 4
Lingual gyrus	L	24	3.39	3.31	-14, -58, 0
Calcarine cortex	R		3.49	3.41	20, -62, 12

Note. H = hemisphere. Uncorrected level of significance level p = .001. Coordinates are given in mm.

Appendix II

Additional tables for study 2 are presented.

Table A6

Main effects and interactions of the mixed ANOVA (Pillai-Spur) of the average empathic judgements in study 2.

Factors	$F_{(1,28)}$	p	η_p^2
condition	1.776	.193	0.060
condition x group	1.721	.200	0.058
valence	2.345	.137	0.077
valence x group	1.176	.287	0.040
congruency	2.277	.143	0.075
congruency x group	2.379	.134	0.078
condition x valence	0.953	.337	0.033
condition x valence x group	1.498	.231	0.051
condition x congruency	7.205	.012	0.205
condition x congruency x group	0.220	.643	0.008
valence x congruency	0.161	.691	0.006
valence x congruency x group	0.015	.904	0.001
condition x valence x congruency	4.968	.034	0.151
condition x valence x congruency x group	0.427	.519	0.015

Note. The ANOVA was calculated with the within-subject factors condition (active vs. passive), valence (inclusion vs. exclusion) and congruency (congruent vs. incongruent), and the between-subjects factor group (Control vs. ASD). Level of significance: $p < .05$.

Table A7
Main effects and interactions of the mixed ANOVA (Pillai-Spur) of the average empathic judgements in study 2 with alexithymia as a covariate.

Factors	$F_{(1,27)}$	p	η_p^2
condition	1.717	.201	0.060
condition x alexithymia	0.075	.786	0.003
condition x group	1.301	.264	0.046
valence	2.513	.125	0.085
valence x alexithymia	3.006	.094	0.100
valence x group	0.110	.742	0.004
congruency	2.385	.134	0.008
congruency x alexithymia	2.329	.139	0.079
congruency x group	4.815	.037	0.151
condition x valence	0.947	.339	0.034
condition x valence x alexithymia	0.846	.366	0.030
condition x valence x group	0.082	.776	0.003
condition x congruency	7.433	.011	0.216
condition x congruency x alexithymia	1.883	.181	0.065
condition x congruency x group	0.323	.574	0.012
valence x congruency	0.160	.692	0.006
valence x congruency x alexithymia	0.853	.364	0.031
valence x congruency x group	0.281	.600	0.010
condition x valence x congruency	4.791	.037	0.151

(continued)

Table A7
Main effects and interactions of the mixed ANOVA (Pillai-Spur) of the average empathic judgements in study 2 with alexithymia as a covariate (continued).

Factors	$F_{(1,27)}$	p	η_p^2
condition x valence x congruency x alexithymia	0.005	.924	< 0.001
condition x valence x congruency x group	0.182	.673	0.007

Note. The ANOVA was calculated with the within-subject factors condition (active vs. passive), valence (inclusion vs. exclusion) and congruency (congruent vs. incongruent), and the between-subjects factor group (Control vs. ASD). Alexithymia was mean-centered and put into the model as a covariate. Level of significance: $p < .05$.

Table A8
Main effects and interactions of the mixed ANOVA (Pillai-Spur) of the average empathic judgements in study 2 with autistic traits as a covariate.

Factors	$F_{(1,27)}$	p	η_p^2
condition	1.794	.192	0.062
condition x autistic traits	1.288	.266	0.046
condition x group	2.787	.107	0.094
valence	2.351	.137	0.080
valence x autistic traits	1.073	.309	0.038
valence x group	0.078	.782	0.003
congruency	2.244	.146	0.077
congruency x autistic traits	0.593	.448	0.021
congruency x group	2.187	.151	0.075
condition x valence	0.919	.346	0.033
condition x valence x autistic traits	0.011	.916	< 0.001
condition x valence x group	0.552	.464	0.020

(continued)

Table A8
Main effects and interactions of the mixed ANOVA (Pillai-Spur) of the average empathic judgements in study 2 with autistic traits as a covariate (continued).

Factors	$F_{(1,27)}$	p	η_p^2
condition x congruency	7.493	.011	0.217
condition x congruency x autistic traits	2.119	.157	0.073
condition x congruency x group	0.925	.345	0.033
valence x congruency	0.158	.694	0.006
valence x congruency x autistic traits	0.540	.469	0.020
valence x congruency x group	0.304	.586	0.011
condition x valence x congruency	4.869	.036	0.153
condition x valence x congruency x autistic traits	0.441	.512	0.016
condition x valence x congruency x group	0.042	.839	0.002

Note. The ANOVA was calculated with the within-subject factors condition (active vs. passive), valence (inclusion vs. exclusion) and congruency (congruent vs. incongruent), and the between-subjects factor group (Control vs. ASD). The level of autistic traits was mean-centered and put into the model as a covariate. Level of significance: $p < .05$.

Table A9

Spearman correlations between the mean EEBs, alexithymia, trait empathy and autistic traits in study 2.

	Controls (n = 15)			ASD (n = 15)		
	Active EEB	Passive EEB	EEB Diff.	Active EEB	Passive EEB	EEB Diff.
Alexithymia						
DIF	-.31	**-.67***	.34	.05	-.23	.27
DDF	.29	.08	-.09	-.04	-.18	.17
EOT	.23	.05	-.09	.22	.29	.11
Overall Score	.01	-.28	-.07	.03	< .01	.15
Trait empathy						
Fantasy	-.27	-.25	-.07	.16	-.35	.22
Empathic Concern	**-.53***	-.35	-.18	.23	**-.56***	**.53***
Perspective Taking	-.34	-.09	-.14	-.25	-.04	-.26
Personal Distress	-.17	-.27	.23	-.09	**-.70***	.44
Autistic traits	.26	-.03	.34	-.09	.06	.13

Note. Correlations were calculated two-sided. The EEB difference was calculated by subtracting the mean passive EEB from the mean active EEB. Significant correlations ($p < .05$) are marked with an asterisk. The sample size for study 1 was $n_2 = 30$. DIF = Difficulty Identifying Feelings, DDF = Difficulty Describing Feelings, EOT = Externally Oriented Thinking.

Table A10

Main effects and interactions of the repeated measures ANOVA (Pillai-Spur) of the average rating time in study 2.

Factors	$F_{(1,28)}$	p	η_p^2
condition	1.158	.291	0.040
condition x group	0.689	.414	0.024
valence	9.505	.005	0.253
valence x group	0.075	.786	0.003
congruency	0.695	.411	0.024
congruency x group	1.884	.181	0.063
condition x valence	2.505	.125	0.082
condition x valence x group	3.605	.068	0.114
condition x congruency	0.618	.438	0.022
condition x congruency x group	1.826	.187	0.061
valence x congruency	1.367	.252	0.047
valence x congruency x group	0.227	.638	0.008
condition x valence x congruency	3.856	.060	0.121
condition x valence x congruency x group	0.236	.631	0.008

Note. The ANOVA was calculated with the within-subject factors condition (active vs. passive), valence (inclusion vs. exclusion) and congruency (congruent vs. incongruent), and the between-subjects factor group (Controls vs. ASD). Level of significance: $p < .05$.

Table A11
Main effect of valence (Other inclusion > exclusion) in study 2.

Anatomical Region	H	cluster K	*p* (unc)	*T*	Z score	x, y, z
Inferior occipital gyrus	R		< .001	4.16	4.08	36, -76, -6
Inferior occipital gyrus	R		< .001	3.89	3.83	30, -82, -10
Superior temporal gyrus	R	68	< .001	4.10	4.02	46, -38, 12
Fusiform gyrus	L	48	< .001	3.43	3.38	-36, -60, -8
Middle temporal gyrus	R	34	< .001	3.38	3.34	52, -52, 16

Note. H = hemisphere. Uncorrected level of significance level $p = .001$. Coordinates are given in mm.

Kolibri 360 GmbH
Ferdinand-Jühlke-Straße 7
99095 Erfurt, Deutschland
produktsicherheit@kolibri360.de